Joesph Conrad's
THE HEART OF DARKNESS

AND
THE SECRET SHARER

JAMES WEISS
DEPARTMENT OF ENGLISH EDUCATION
NEW YORK UNIVERSITY

MONARCH PRESS

Standard Book Number: 671-00817-X
Library of Congress Catalog Card Number: 66-27266

CONTENTS

INTRODUCTION

BEGINNINGS: In 1856 Appolo Korzeniowski, aged 36, and
Ewelina Bobrowska, aged 25, married in Podolia, a Polish prov-
ince under Russian rule. On December 3, 1857, their only child
Teodor Jozef Konrad Korzeniowski was born. In 1862, a little
more than five years after Joseph Conrad's birth, his father moved
the family to Warsaw and launched what was ostensibly a literary magazine called the *Fortnightly Review*. Appolo Korzeniowski was an ardent Polish patriot who resented the Russian
domination of Poland, however, and he used the magazine as
a cover to promote resistance against Russian rule. The secret
National Committee, which he helped to create, met frequently
in his home. Even before the 1863 insurrection in Warsaw
against Russian rule, Conrad's father was arrested and after
ten months detention in the Citadel in Warsaw was exiled to
Russia. Conrad's mother asked for permission to follow Appolo
into exile. Less than three years later, the frail and poverty-
stricken Mrs. Korzeniowski died at the age of thirty-four. After
being released from Russian exile Conrad's father died a mel-
ancholy and defeated person in Cracow, in 1869. The death of
both parents helped to intensify Conrad's own tendencies toward
gloom and introspection and forced him to seek refuge in the
world of books. He was later reared by an aristocratic uncle-
guardian, Thaddeus Bobrowski, who sent him to St. Anne High
School in Cracow, where he studied Latin, German, geography,
and history. It is well to note that both sides of Conrad's family
belonged to the landed gentry and the family history is replete
with men who had important military careers. From his father's
side of the family, Conrad inherited a passionate, romantic nature tinged with revolutionary zeal; from his mother he inherited

a practical, down-to-earth personality housed in a delicate constitution. Both contributed to his development as a writer. Had it not been for his poor health, which prevented him from continuing his career as a seaman, Conrad might never have settled down to the long and cruelly laborious occupation of writing novels.

YOUTH: At the age of fifteen, Conrad announced his ambition to go to sea. His biographer, Gerard Jean-Aubry, believes this ambition reflected Conrad's desire to leave the stifling atmosphere of his school. Jean-Aubry's theory is supported by Conrad's rejection of the idea that he attend a naval academy in Pola, the academy of the Austrian Navy. Conrad preferred to begin his life as a seaman immediately, without further schooling. Clearly, Conrad wanted to leave his schools, his surroundings which reminded him of his dead parents, and the oppressive atmosphere of Poland—a country under the paw of the Russian bear.

Other biographers attribute his desire to leave Poland to quite a different source. It was about this time that the official Polish attitude toward the revolution was being revised. The glorious revolution of 1863 was now considered an inglorious mistake. Conrad's father who had sacrificed so much to bring about the revolution had sacrificed in vain. The rigors of exile which brought an early death to both his parents and a lonely childhood to Conrad himself were consummated in a lamentable repudiation. It is no wonder, according to his biographers, that Conrad found it difficult to remain in a society which rejected the suffering and sacrifice of his family.

Conrad's Uncle Thaddeus attempted to dissuade him from going to sea, but Conrad remained firm. At the age of seventeen, to his guardian's horror, he went to Marseilles, and from there sailed over the world on various respectable and disrespectable expeditions, including gun-running trips to Central and South America. Among his many exploits is a love affair with a Spanish court lady, and a duel fought over her with an American adventurer. Conrad claims that through this lady he became the master of a smuggling ship working for the Carlist pretender.

All this, and much more, occurred before Conrad was twenty-one. Undoubtedly a great deal of Conrad's "autobiography" must be taken with a grain of salt. There is evidence, for example, that the scar with which Conrad always demonstrated his having been wounded in the duel was suffered in a much more prosaic way. It is safe to say that, for purposes of his own, Conrad seems to have purposely desired that his early life at sea be permanently shrouded in mystery. Nevertheless, it is absolutely clear what the sea meant to the young Conrad: "After a childhood weighed down by oppression, how excellent and moving it was to be free from social conventions and political tyranny, alone, and face to face with the wide spaces of the sea!" Young Powell in *Chance* utters these words but we may feel comfortable in saying that Conrad himself shared this attitude toward the sea.

THE BRITISH NAVY: At the age of twenty-one Conrad became committed to the idea of being an English master mariner. He studied the language from newspapers and books, and on April 24, 1878, he shipped out for Constantinople on the English steamer, the *Mavis*. He had decided, as he points out in *A Personal Record,* that if he was to be a seaman, he would be an English seaman and no other. After two years in the British service he passed his examination for third mate and in 1883 and 1886, for mate and master. Once he had made his decision, curiously enough, he became almost more British than the British themselves. He subscribed wholeheartedly, or at least he tried to subscribe, to the ethic of unquestioning duty that was characteristic of the Imperial Navy. From that time onward he stayed away from illegal adventures and was known as an excellent sailor, if one somewhat too prone to take chances.

From January, 1888, to March, 1889, he had command of his first ship, the *Otago.* The story of his first voyage can be read in *The Shadow-Line,* possibly the most autobiographical of all his works. He continued in Her Majesty's Merchant Marine for several years, mostly in the Far East. That area, particularly the Malayan archipelago, became the location for many of his novels and stories.

APPRENTICESHIP-TO-LIFE: It is impossible to overestimate the importance this learning period had for Conrad. In story after story he reveals how difficult it is to bridge the gap between youth and manhood, between wanton, adventuresome living and commitment to a mature responsible ideal. The theme of initiation does not refer only to adolescence facing manhood; in Conrad man is always an apprentice to the dark imponderables within life and within himself. The ordeal of initiation is shared by men of all ages as they progress out of their egotism and move to a more comprehensive morality. In the young, however, the ordeal is more clear-cut and the emergence more immediately satisfying. In his short story, "Youth," the idea of apprenticing and emergence is most clearly delineated in its purest, albeit elemental, form. Later on in *The Secret Sharer* and *Heart of Darkness* we shall see the deeper implications of emergence and non-emergence.

LITERARY BEGINNINGS: Not until his thirties did Conrad begin writing. His first novel, *Almayer's Folly,* was begun on shore leave in London, and continued for several years on various ships. Much of it was written on the flyleaves of his copy of Flaubert's *Madame Bovary*. It was published in 1895, the year after he gave up life at sea in favor of a literary career. Though showing a number of faults as a novel, *Almayer's Folly* revealed the characteristics of a serious craftsman and stylist. His second novel, *An Outcast of the Islands* (1896), was a continuation of the history of certain characters in *Almayer's Folly*. In 1897 he published his first really major work, *The Nigger of the Narcissus*. The ten years following the publication of *The Nigger of the Narcissus* saw one of the greatest creative outbursts, not only in Conrad's life but in all modern literature. Many of his most memorable works were written during this period, including *Lord Jim* (1900), *Typhoon* and *Heart of*

Darkness (1902), *Nostromo* (1904), and *The Secret Agent* (1907). *The Secret Sharer* was published in 1910.

LATER SUCCESS: Most critics feel that after this decade, or at least after *Under Western Eyes* (1911), the quality of Conrad's work dropped considerably. With the exceptions of *Victory* (1914) and *The Shadow Line* (1917), no one of his later works is considered a major work. It is ironic that Conrad's popular success arrived at precisely the time when his artistic powers began to decline. Prior to 1913, when he had his first great commercial success with *Chance,* he had been virtually unrecognized by the public. From that date, however, he became one of the most sought after writers of England. His popularity steadily increased until his death (1924), some eleven years later, at the age of sixty-seven.

CONRAD'S LANGUAGE: What has made Conrad one of the most difficult of writers in English is not the complexity of his thought, which indeed appears difficult enough, but his rhetoric or language style. Both his language and the construction of his books create great problems for the reader. A certain part of our difficulty with his language may be due to the fact that he did not learn English until the age of twenty. French was his second tongue and many of his expressions strike us •as highly gallicized. Some of his passages even look as if they had been translated from the French. He loved to use balanced phrases and parallel structure in his sentences. Often he interrupted his narrative to give long, poetic descriptions of natural scenes. While his purpose in such passages is to help create the proper tone and atmosphere for the story, some critics complain that his verbosity diminishes the accumulation of tension and prevents the reader from becoming unalterably involved with the events.

Conrad's prose is always heightened. His word choice, the rhythm of his phrasing, the length of his sentences, the paragraph climaxes, all conspire to lift his prose to the level of eloquence, to a premeditatedly heightened level which produces a kind of intoxication. When successful, this state of raptness works on the reader to make him receptive to the meanings embedded in the overall pattern of the story. The language is loaded and impressive especially when the concrete presentation of incident and natural setting provide a context for the language to illuminate. However, as Leavis points out in his controversial set of essays, *The Great Tradition,* Conrad's language becomes an excrescence when it is imposed on the reader without the validation of objective experience. It is as if Conrad were trying to convince the reader solely through his language that something important was taking place. When Conrad is trying to invoke in the reader a feeling for the vague and unrealizable, he intensifies his language and insists on the existence of something powerful and mysterious because he can't really produce that intensity through the event. One should be on his guard when Conrad uses the terms "indefinable," "exotic," "inconceivable," "enigmatic," "inscrutable"; he is probably trying too hard to invest the experience with significance. Leavis compares this tendency towards "thrilled insistency" with the melodramatic intensities of Edgar Allen Poe. When Conrad is writing badly, as he often does in his later works, his language becomes murky and pretentious. Often it is hard to know whether it is the obscurity of the language or the density of the reader that is causing the difficulty. R. P. Blackmur identifies this misuse of language as the fallacy of expressive form: the belief that if a thing is felt deeply enough its expression in language will automatically give it satisfactory form. The error implied in this fallacy is that the writer abdicates his formal obligation to the raw material of his subject matter. Overstatement can be one of Conrad's effective literary devices; it can also betray a specious reality.

SYMBOLISM: In all his works, Conrad's main objective is the presentation of a psychological and moral reality, rather than an external naturalism. In attempting to describe the various mental states of his characters, Conrad resorts to the use of symbolism. His books are invariably built around a symbolic skeleton, which reveals the psychological attributes of his characters better than anything "realistic" could do. In fact, his choice and repetitious use of various natural elements in some of his stories lends a sort of super-reality to the narrative. When the conclusion of *Victory* draws near, for example, there is a violent thunderstorm. This indicates to the reader that the judgment of heaven is about to descend.

Conrad also employs objects, both natural and man-made, with great success as symbols. The ever thickening jungle in the *Heart of Darkness,* the white hat in *The Secret Sharer,* the silver mine in *Nostromo* are all examples. All of them are symbolic stand-ins for the thoughts and emotions of the characters as well as for supervening embodiments of the thematic message. Consider the title of the *Heart of Darkness.* On a strictly literal level these words could be interpreted to represent the outline of the continent of Africa which does indeed resemble a crude sketch of a human heart. The skin tone of Africans fulfills the total symbolism inherent in the *Heart of Darkness.* But "heart" can also be taken to mean the place of central importance, of most vital significance. And when the center is a repository of "darkness," the symbolism suggests a form of hellishness producing dark thoughts and actions. Another possible interpretation of "darkness" is that of ambiguity, things not clearly seen. So the title may prefigure a story of mystery and veiled truths. The permutations are endless.

DELIBERATE AMBIGUITY: Conrad's use of language and symbol are joined in a single key image that occurs abundantly in the two stories we shall examine; this image is the shadow. Often the shadow is accompanied by such images as mist, fog, cloud, darkness, and blackness; it is opposed by various images of light: candlelight, moonlight, sunlight, and lightning flashes. Through this central image, the shadow, Conrad comments on the world around him and on the people in it. If the world of light, daytime, and consciousness exists on the surface of Conrad's thinking, then the world of darkness, ambiguity, and shadow exists beneath the surface, beneath the conscious level of things—exists in the subconscious itself.

Another device that Conrad habitually uses to blur the straight reportorial picture of reality is the use of multiple narrators. Narrative viewpoints change abruptly, often several times in a chapter. The traditional straightforward chronological sequence is destroyed by constantly skipping back and forth through time. Often we seem to be floating in time, not quite certain of when the events being described are taking place. This technique at first promises utter befuddlement. One craves a single reliable commentator talking in a comprehensible time sequence about what really is going on. Later on, however, as we total up the impressions received from disparate personalities and untangle the convoluted sequences of narrative we find ourselves in possession of a deeper, more comprehensive reality. We conclude by understanding the story far better than we would have had Conrad limited himself to a conventional narrative style.

THEORY OF DOUBLES: THE DOPPELGANGER: Of all Conrad's methods of portraying the inner life of his characters, one stands out as the most original and the most successful: the double. In his works, a double is a person who stands for a characteristic or emotion in another person. Sometimes the identification may be complete; sometimes it is only partial. It may be an older man seeing himself in a younger one, or it may be two people very close in age. The clearest example of such a figure is found in *The Secret Sharer*. In that story the hero actually hides another man, who is an embodiment of his own fears and guilt, on board his ship. They struggle throughout the symbolic voyage, until the hero learns to recognize the ugly, violent qualities his double represents and is able at the end to accept his baser nature and free the double. In the *Heart of Darkness,* Kurtz may be regarded as representing the evil suppressed within Marlowe. The confrontation between them in the jungle is then seen as an intra-psychic struggle taking place within Marlowe rather than a contest between two distinctly separate personalities. In *The Nigger of the Narcissus,* the Negro, James Wait, serves as a collective double for all the ordinary seamen. He, too, represents the worst part of their personalities. We should note, though, that such a device would always fail if it were not for the masterful way in which Conrad makes his doubles real as well as symbolic. James

Wait exists as an unpleasant, shirking, whining Jamaican, before he functions as a symbol. It is only because he is so real that we can accept him as having more than natural significance.

THREE KINDS OF NOVELS: Conrad's novels can be conveniently divided into three categories, although all three overlap quite often. These are the jungle novels, the sea stories, and the novels of politics. Such novels as *Lord Jim* and *Heart of Darkness* fall in the first category. The second includes the famous group of short novels about the sea such as *The Secret Sharer* and *The Shadow Line*. The third category, novels of politics, is headed by *Nostromo,* and includes such works as *The Secret Agent* and *Under Western Eyes*.

THE JUNGLE NOVELS: These novels generally focus on a single individual, usually a white man, who, for one reason or another, has chosen to isolate himself from white society and live in a primitive fashion. In *Victory*, Heyst isolates himself from the civilization he has known in England because he is disillusioned with its corruption and complexity. Jim, in *Lord Jim,* feels that he has committed an unforgivable moral crime by deserting his ship and he cannot face the world again because of his act of cowardice. In every case, the individual is unable to escape the real world, which intrudes into his hideaway often in the form of renegades seeking plunder. Conrad is primarily interested in the moral and psychological problems that arise from the invasion of the hero's private world. His heroes have forsworn any intercourse with the world, but Conrad forces them to face it. They must pass through extreme emotional crises before they can be redeemed and become morally whole human beings again. Many of Conrad's characters pay for the redemption with their lives, making their stories essentially tragic quests.

THE SEA STORIES: The great sea stories, *The Nigger of the Narcissus, Typhoon, Youth, The Shadow-Line,* and *The Secret Sharer* are all short novels. They all deal with the sea as a character in itself. The backgrounds become vitally important in these novels. The sea is almost a moral force, against which the men in the stories are eventually judged. The stories customarily concern a voyage, which is not only a real voyage, but a voyage of the soul as well. The two trips are intimately connected. The storms and calms which beset the sailors are reflections of the storms and calms in their souls. While he is waiting for a favorable wind, the new captain in *The Secret Sharer* is beset with real doubt about his voyage as well as spiritual uncertainty about the assumption of his first command. He, as well as the ship, is becalmed.

Conrad's sea tales are masterpieces on the level of adventure stories as well. No other writer in English has been able to capture the feeling of the sea and ships as has Conrad. Every line of the tales shows that they have been written by a man with a complete and sensitive awareness of nautical life. In fact, toward the end of his life, Conrad became known to the public exclusively as a writer of sea stories. He once said that he almost wished he had never written them, so that people would take his work as seriously as it deserved to be taken.

THE POLITICAL NOVELS: The political novels are somewhat less concerned with the moral problems of people confined within themselves and unable to flee from a spiritual day of reckoning. Rather, they deal, especially in *Nostromo,* with the facts of the entire society and with people who are in the deepest sense cut off yet remain vitally connected with societal imperatives. In *Nostromo,* Conrad invents an entire country and creates a particular, unique social, geographical, and historical structure. In this mythical society Conrad brings into play all the variegated forces that are shaping the modern world and which in turn shape the destinies of the individual characters in the novel. The country itself is the real subject, not in its physical or geographical context, but in its human constitution. The lust for silver is the "pivot of the moral and material events, affecting the lives of everybody in the tale." Silver is in the land, but the lust for it is in the people. It is the general picture of the citizens and their various lives—the interaction among them and the contest against the background environment— which is of primary importance in this novel. Again, one can interpret Conrad's political novels as adventure stories excitingly reported, but if one were to limit these novels to the level of reportage one would miss Conrad's attempt to display the deeper forces structuring all of Western society.

CONRAD'S ARTISTIC MANIFESTO: In the Preface to his novel *The Nigger of the Narcissus* Conrad wrote of his aesthetic goals in writing fiction. He stated that the conscience of the artist is more important than the formulas dictated by certain acceptable styles. In order to be truly convincing, the writer must convey his impression through the senses—"the secret spring of responsive emotions." Each line of prose has the responsibility of carrying the conviction of truth. The artist must reveal the dynamics of the whole within the core of each particular moment. By perfectly blending form and substance, the writer can make the audience perceive a throbbing, living reality. "My task which I am trying to achieve is, by the power of the written word, to make you hear, to make you feel—it is, before all, to make you *see*. That—and no more, and it is everything."

CONRAD'S INFLUENCE: During his lifetime Conrad was acclaimed for his achievement as a master storyteller. However, not many critics at the time had the prescience to understand how deeply his method and meaning would influence writers in the future. Although accused of being a Victorian in disguise, Conrad preempts some of the major themes which have obsessed writers of fiction throughout this century. Hemingway's articulation of the failure of any kind of abstraction, no matter how ideal, to serve the well-being of humanity is an echo of Kurtz's failure of idealism in the Congo. In a kindred fashion Fitzgerald's famous failure, Gatsby, is a perverted relative in misguided idealism. Woolf and Joyce, accompanied by a host of others, have advanced Conrad's technique of multiple narration moving back and forth through time. What was ambiguous in Conrad has been refined into techniques of deliberate mystification and obscurity.

Conrad's major contribution is probably his quest for inner certitude in a world bent on external acquisition. Progress is an empty "happening" if it is not founded on a moral base. His desperate, intense search for ethical conduct in the face of exploding materialism provides an enduring frame for most of twentieth-century fiction.

HEART OF DARKNESS

INTRODUCTION

In September of 1889, Conrad began writing his first novel, *Almayer's Folly*, but he was more interested in beginning an adventure which was to provide material for one of his most widely read works, *Heart of Darkness*. Years before, in 1868, when he was a boy of nine, Conrad had been staring at a map of Africa. Pointing with his finger to the blank space that was then the unexplored heart of the continent, he said, "When I grow up I shall go *there*." Now, twenty-one years later and in a different country, Conrad decided to make good on his boyhood promise. The blank space on the map of Africa was no longer blank; it was the Belgian Congo. Conrad decided to ask for the job of captain on one of the steamers that plied the river which leads into the center of that territory.

Thus, in September of 1889, a letter was presented to Albert Thys, acting head of the Sociéte Anonyme Belge pour les Commerce du Haut-Congo, recommending Captain Korzeniowski for the job. In January of 1890, he wrote to an aunt by marriage, Madame Marguerite Poradowska, asking her to see what she could do to help him to obtain his appointment. Madame Poradowska was a woman of thirty, beautiful and surrounded by a circle of influential friends. If anyone in Brussels could help Conrad, she could. On the fifth of February, Conrad began a trip from England to the Ukraine, where he was to visit relatives. He stopped off in Brussels to see Madame Poradowska, and then continued his trip. He spent several months in the

Ukraine, but he corresponded with Madame Poradowska about his hoped-for job. Finally, on April 29, 1890, Conrad arrived for a second time in Brussels, this time to sign a contract to act as a riverboat pilot on the Congo River in Africa. On May 11, 1890, he set out for Bordeaux, France, where he would get a boat that would carry him off to Africa. The story of how he got to Africa that Marlowe tells in *Heart of Darkness* is almost exactly the same in its important details as the experience that Conrad had in 1889-1890. After Conrad's death, his literary executors discovered two of the novelist's notebooks from the period when he had gone into the Congo. These along with an accompanying essay by his friend, Richard Curle, were published in the volume *Last Essays* in 1926. Anyone who goes to the trouble of comparing these notebooks to *Heart of Darkness* comes to the conclusion that Conrad was working very closely indeed from his actual experiences. Places and people mentioned in *Heart of Darkness* have direct counterparts in the notebooks. Kurtz, for example, seems to have been a man named Georges-Antoine Klein. (Klein in German means small, Kurtz means short, brief.) The illness of which Marlowe speaks was real too; Conrad almost died as a result of it.

Despite the biographical verisimilitude, it is crucial to note that Marlowe's voyage into Africa also parallels a spiritual voyage Conrad was making at the same time. Conrad once told Edward Garnett, "Before the Congo I was just a mere animal." In a sense Marlowe/Conrad embark together on a longer kind of journey: a "Pilgrim's Progress" into the self.

PLOT ANALYSIS

PART I: TOWARD THE HEART OF DARKNESS

To the four other men on the deck of the *Nellie,* which is anchored in the Thames, Captain Marlowe proposes to tell of an adventure that happened to him years ago. Before he begins his story, he thinks about the history of England at the time when it was a backward, "underdeveloped" country and Roman soldiers came to it for conquest and plunder.

COMMENT: Conrad wishes us to compare England two thousand years ago to Africa in the nineteenth century. Just as Marlowe is about to travel into the heart of a wilderness, so the Roman soldiers traveled into the heart of a wilderness. An accident of time separates Marlowe from those Roman soldiers. In his ironic prologue, Marlowe says about London, "the biggest, and the greatest, town on earth," that this also, "has been one of the dark places of the earth." Perhaps Conrad is suggesting that the veneer of civilization merely covers the primitive foundation which gives structure to any society, whether it be in England in prehistoric time, Africa in the nineteenth century, or, by extension, America in the twentieth century.

The Narrative Technique: *Heart of Darkness* is written as a narrative within a narrative. The first narrator, some say Conrad himself, never enters the story; he merely describes events that occur on the deck of a yacht. It is Marlowe who narrates the adventures in the Congo. From time to time, the scene moves back to the deck of the yacht, and the first narrator picks up the story.

Why has Conrad gone to the trouble of introducing a character, Marlowe, between the story to be told and the author, Conrad himself? One possibility is that Conrad felt he needed an additional character, not identified with the "pilgrims" (Conrad's ironic name for the agents of the Sociéte . . . Haut-Congo) of the trading company, nor with the author himself. The function of this character would be to establish a norm against whom we can compare the actions of the other characters. Marlowe stands for Man as he usually is, while the "pilgrims" and Kurtz stand for Man when he deviates from the norm.

But upon close analysis of the text in this opening section, the character of Marlowe offers us something more than an embodiment of standards and normative behavior by which we measure the eccentricity of the other characters. We first encounter him sitting "cross-legged," with "sunken cheeks" and an "ascetic aspect" resembling an idol. He does not "represent his class"; he was not "typical." Although he shares the sailor's propensity for telling tales, Marlowe does not believe that meaning in life is so easily extracted as cracking a nut and removing the kernel; for him the meaning lies outside the nut, in the atmosphere enveloping the tale, in the spectral illumination sometimes provided by moonlight.

Marlowe, at the end of the opening section, is seated Buddha-like in the Lotus position preaching to his listeners. His moralizing about conquest is pointed: "The conquest of the earth, which mostly means the taking it away from those who have a different complexion or slightly flatter noses than ourselves, is not a pretty thing when you look into too much." Conquest is only vindicated by the idealistic notion that the conquered may one day benefit from the civilizing of the conquerors. What this idealism in fact produces is Marlowe's "inconclusive experience." Initially, then, Marlowe is three things: a narrative device to vary the boredom of listening to a single authorial voice, a moral philosopher intent on bringing things into true perspective, a vital participant in these events whose own life stands as testimony to the ironies of life.

It is vital to note that there are five people seated on board the *Nellie,* the two narrators and the Lawyer, the Accountant, and the Director of Companies. The triumvirate who are defined by their job titles offer us another level of perception about life—later on in the story we shall see what they have to say about Conrad's tale. The "I" or the personality of the author also must react, and does, to Marlowe's tale, even though he sometimes takes a hand in relating the story. It is precisely this differentiating of point of view which allows Conrad to point to meanings without becoming didactic.

Light and Dark: If one were to take the trouble to count, one would notice an astonishing number of references, in the first four pages of this story, to degrees of light and dark. Things are not clearly seen nor are they yet invisible. The story starts in twilight between a luminous river and a gloomy dark city; the game the group prepares to play but never does play is dominoes—white dots on black rectangles. Even after the sun sets, new lights appear along the shore irradiating the darkness. This atmospheric flickering underscores the psychological mystery Marlowe finds at the "culminating point" of his experience. He too is undecided about the clarity or meaning of this experience; it was sombre, not very clear, and yet it seemed to throw some kind of light. This can be taken to mean that ultimately we will not be told anything in a definitive manner; in the wilderness, both external and inner, there is a detestable wildness which is both abominable and fascinating.

Marlowe describes how he came to make the trip to the Congo. He was a young man out of a job; he had been interested in the Congo for a long time; he had an aunt who could help him to get an appointment as a river-boat pilot. In short,

Marlowe retells the story that Conrad had actually experienced. After being examined by a doctor, who measures his "crania," he takes a French steamer to the mouth of the Congo River. The steamer has made many stops along the way and Marlowe is impressed with the sameness of the jungle landscape, and the mysteriousness of it. They pass a French gunboat firing shells into the jungle. Marlowe is told that there are natives in the jungle, but the idea is apparently ludicrous to him (as if one could shoot the jungle, as the Roman emperor tried to beat the sea because it would not obey his commands).

> **COMMENT:** The idea of progress is sarcastically underlined. The emissary of progress, the medical man, uses phrenology to measure a man's psychological fitness. His aunt sees him as an "emissary of light" who should wean "those ignorant millions from their horrid ways." But Marlowe perceives "how out of touch with truth women are." He, instead, is being prepared for inward progress of a dangerous kind. Belgium is a "sepulchre": the two women at the entrance to the Company's offices are knitting black wool, foreshadowing as it were a dangerous descent; the doctor understands that his measurements are futile, "the changes take place inside, you know." The only secure factors in this adventure are the paddling natives who "wanted no excuse for being there."

Finally, the steamer reaches the mouth of the Congo and Marlowe disembarks. He boards a smaller steamer, this one commanded by a Swedish captain, and starts on the first leg of his journey up the river. Before Marlowe leaves the Swede, he is told about another Swede who hanged himself; apparently, the jungle has a dangerous effect on the people who travel in it. Marlowe leaves the Swedish captain at the Company Station. The station is hardly the model of efficiency that one might expect. In fact, we are told only of the broken machinery, the useless effort, the dying natives, and one strangely incongruous dandy, complete with starched collar and polished boots. It is the dandy, the company accountant, who first tells Marlowe of Kurtz.

COMMENT: In this first encounter with the borders of the jungle existence, Marlowe senses encroaching irrationality. The slaves are busy detonating a mountain to make way for a railway which will skirt the mountain anyway. The slaves, manacled together in an unfamiliar environment, cannot produce efficiently. Only the accountant seems to have things "in apple-pie order"; only the numbers, those closed systems of abstractions, with which he records the arrival of the precious ivory, make coherent sense.

The Accountant: The accountant serves two purposes. Through him we first discover the "remarkable" presence of Kurtz, who somewhere in the interior has been able to ship. more ivory than any other company agent. The effect of this information is to create a mystery about Kurtz rather than to make him a clearly drawn character. Great things are predicted for Kurtz by the "Council of Europe," but we don't know why. Secondly, the accountant serves as a model for survival in life. By "keeping up appearances" in a demoralized atmosphere, by not giving in to sloth and apathy, he is a victor of sorts and has "backbone." Doing one's duty in the face of powerful odds is an important factor in Conrad's code of right behavior.

Marlowe continues his journey up the river. In the jungle he sees further signs of the inefficiency and chaos that pervade the story. He comes upon the body of a native, shot through the forehead; remembering his conversation with the company doctor, Marlowe thinks he is becoming "scientifically interesting," that is, going insane. Along the path are abandoned native villages; the dismal countryside has been deserted. At the end of fifteen days of walking through the jungle, Marlowe reaches the Central Station. There Marlowe meets the company manager who does not invite him to sit down. Instead he confronts Marlowe with yet another obstacle; the steamer which he is to pilot is at the bottom of the river. Not only must Marlowe raise the steamer and repair the bottom, but he must do it without the proper tools because, inexplicably, no rivets can be found upstream, although they lay strewn all over the station two hundred miles down the river. In all, it will be three months before the steamer is repaired and Marlowe can start upstream on the next leg of his journey. A shed mysteriously bursts into flame one night. One of the company employees attempts to fight the fire, but he fails to notice that the pail he is using has a hole in the bottom. Such is the inefficiency of Europeans in Africa. The narrative is sharply interrupted at this point with the words, "He was silent for a while."

COMMENT: Here is the first of several occasions where the mysterious, unnamed first narrator on the deck of the *Nellie* back in London breaks in upon Marlowe's narrative. In our imaginations we jump several decades and several thousand miles from one paragraph to the next. Such a shift reminds us of the fictional nature of the story we are reading while the details and direct experience given to us by Marlowe convince us of the truth of the fiction. Thus we have two opposing forces at work, reality and fiction, which generate a tension within the tale. The "story-within-a-story" technique in fiction is very much like framing a painting with an ornate frame. The frame helps us to distinguish between the painting and the surface upon which it hangs (our living-room wall, for instance). At the same time, if the framing is artistically achieved, the picture's qualities will be properly focused and enhanced. So the literary framework, the first of the two narratives, helps us to distinguish between what is happening in the Congo, and what is happening around us in the living-room of our lives. It is the artist's hope that this fluctuation between his fiction and our reality will result in changing our perceptions about the world.

The Company Manager: Later on in the story Marlowe will discuss his "choice of nightmares." It has been stated that one of the choices is naturally Kurtz and the other is the choice inherent in the way of life of the company manager. There is nothing spectacular or complex about the manager, but he does inspire a sort of admiration for being able to survive in an environment in which there were no "external checks." Marlowe attributes his ability "to keep the routine going" to his empty inner life; the manager is truly a hollow man devoid of entrails. He does his job but so does a machine. Marlowe considers the job of work as an opportunity for finding out about himself; work per se is not an ennobling thing. The manager has a kind of alter ego, the brickmaker. Marlowe calls him a "papier-maché Mephistopheles" who serves absolutely no purpose in the wilderness because there are no bricks to make. It is purposelessness which can be nightmarish and Marlowe recognizes that if he chooses this way of living, he has chosen a form of death-in-life. Thus, in this case by presenting an alternative in Kurtz, Conrad allows us to find out a little more about the "universal genius." It is ironic comment that a picture Kurtz has painted, an enigmatic panel of a blindfolded woman carrying a lighted torch, is discovered by Marlowe in the brickmaker's home.

The first part of the narrative draws to a conclusion with additional information about Kurtz and additional comment on the "pilgrims."

COMMENT: Apparently, there are two kinds of "pilgrims": there are the "pilgrims" who are in Africa to make a fortune, and there are the "pilgrims" who are there with a sense of mission. This mission translates into something like the "white man's burden" for us today, but in the late nineteenth century the idea probably carried less stigma; then the sense of mission might have been a little more tolerable than it is now. Kurtz seems to be one of the "new men," that is, he is an idealist motivated by humane concerns. He is also extremely successful: no one ships more ivory to the coast than he. His success bothers the profit-motivated "pilgrims" because they feel their own position in the company is being challenged. The introductory section ends with the arrival of a rapacious collection of white men known as the Eldorado Exploration Expedition. These people— "greedy without audacity, and cruel without courage"— endure only to rip treasure from the bowels of the earth.

They are led, coincidentally enough, by a man who was the manager's uncle, a man who resembles "a butcher in a poor neighborhood." The choice for Marlowe is clear—he must find Kurtz and speak with him.

PART II: IN THE HEART OF DARKNESS

Part I opened with Marlowe on deck, the deck of the *Nellie* in London; Part II opens with him on another deck, the deck of the little river-boat at the Company Station, several hundred miles up the river in the Congo. While he is lying on the deck one evening, the chief agent strolls by in the company of his uncle, who is leading the Eldorado Exploring Expedition. They stop alongside the boat, which has been drawn up upon the river bank to be repaired; and unaware of Marlowe's presence, they begin to discuss Kurtz. They recall how, one year ago, Kurtz started down the river with a shipment of ivory. After travelling three hundred miles, Kurtz turned back with only four oarsmen in a single canoe. Even though he was out of supplies with which to trade with the natives for ivory, he decided to go back. Why has he done this? Marlowe imagines that Kurtz returned because he was "a fine fellow who stuck to his work for its own sake."

COMMENT: This section further reinforces the division between the "pilgrims." Kurtz, the "pilgrim" with a mission, is clearly differentiated from the other "pilgrims." This information, it is important to recognize, is purposely presented to us from the point of view of the marauder "pilgrims," thus investing the contrast with a certain layer of probability.

The interview between the chief agent and his uncle is abruptly cut short when they realize that Marlowe is on the deck of the river-boat listening to their conversation. The two men have been discussing the pretentious moralizing of Kurtz; also they have noted that there is a high mortality rate among the white agents in the Congo. The uncle says that one can trust the jungle to take care of killing off the agents. He gestures toward the jungle, taking in with his "flipper"-like arm the river, the sunlight, and the shadow made by the edge of the forest. Marlowe, who has been listening and watching, is so startled by the sight of the jungle that he jumps to his feet.

COMMENT: Why is Marlowe so startled by the appearance of the jungle? Marlowe has been wakened from dozing when the two men started to talk beneath the deck of his beached boat and it is the sudden contrast between the blackness of the jungle and the brilliant sunlit surface that amazes him. Here is an instance of Conrad's use of a physical reality— the drowsy awakening—to underscore a psychological reality—the malevolence of men. Marlowe says that he expected the jungle to make some answer to the two men. He himself tries to offer an explanation for his own startled reaction to the jungle. Instead the jungle becomes personally malevolent to him too. It became a land of "lurking death, . . . hidden evil . . . profound darkness." By personifying the jungle with the dark capabilities of the human heart, and by forcing Marlowe to react against this perception in a semi-conscious state, Conrad intimates symbolically that what is externally dark may have its inner unconscious counterpart.

The river-boat is finally repaired, and a group of "pilgrims," led by the chief agent, begins the trip up the river to Kurtz's station. In all, the trip will take them two months. Marlowe, of course, is the pilot of the boat, and he has a party of twenty cannibals for a crew. They must chop wood to be used as fuel for the boat. As the boat progresses up the river, Marlowe is consistently impressed by the primitive nature of the country around him. He compares the trip up the river to a trip back into time, back to the beginning of time itself.

COMMENT: We are reminded, at this point, of Marlowe's statement at the very beginning of the story. He imagined what a Roman soldier, fresh from the civilization of Rome, must have felt as he travelled up the then primitive Thames.

Marlowe insists upon the mysterious nature of the trip up the river. The jungle, he says, in all its silence seemed to be a brooding, sinister force. All of his attention was taken up by the daily job of avoiding snags and rocks in the river that would sink the boat. The strain of constantly attending to the physical signs around him has a strange effect on Marlowe: the physical world begins to seem unreal, and he is aware of another kind of presence, one that watches him as it watches those who are listening to him. He refers to his listeners aboard the *Nellie* as "tight-rope" walkers. Once again Marlowe's tale is interrupted by a voice from one of his auditors. "Try to be civil, Marlowe," the voice warns.

> **COMMENT:** Again, our imagination must make a sudden shift: from the Congo to the Thames; from the past to the present; from the wilderness to the center of "enlightened" civilization. In addition, we cannot fail to notice the irony in the choice of the word "civil." The listener, whoever he may be, objects to Marlowe's analogy; he prefers that Marlowe be proper and *civilized*. In effect, he rejects any identification with barbarism either in the Congo or hidden under the façade of London civilization.

Marlowe does not reject the identification with savagery. As the river-boat goes deeper and deeper into the heart of the continent, Marlowe identifies with preliterate humanity. He wonders at the primitive people who live along the shore of the river. To Marlowe, the most wonderful thing about them is that, despite their savagery, they are human. More than that, it is wonderful to realize that we too are savage, in the same way that these primitives are, but we have learned to conceal our savagery. In a sense, continues Marlowe, we have, in our own minds buried the experience of our collective pasts.

> **COMMENT:** More remarkable than Marlowe's understanding of the nature of primitive people, both civilized and un-

civilized, is the appearance here of ideas we have come to associate with the mystical psychiatry of Carl Jung. Jung published his theories of the "collective unconscious" and the continuance of cultural history (that is, the inheritance of certain cultural ideas which occurs in the same way as the inheritance of the color of our eyes) long after Conrad wrote *Heart of Darkness*.

Fifty miles below Kurtz's station, Marlowe and the "pilgrims" discover a ruined hut prepared with fire wood already cut and stacked for them. A note contains a plea for help and a warning. While the cannibals and the "pilgrims" load the wood onto the boat, Marlowe investigates the ruined hut. Within, he discovers a book, *An Inquiry into Some Points of Seamanship*. It is obvious that the book has been well used: the pages are very soiled, the covers have come off and extensive notes have been written in the margins, apparently in code.

> **COMMENT:** Marlowe is amazed, and delighted, to discover this sign of civilization and of order in the wilderness—it showed "an honest concern for the right way of going to work." He has noticed nothing but chaos and disorder for the hundreds of miles he has travelled in the Congo. Now he suddenly comes across a seaman's manual, an English book, hundreds of miles from the sea and thousands of miles from England. It seems to him like running into an old friend.

The manager remarks that an illusive renegade trader must have left the wood for them. Thus, with a new mystery, Marlowe guides his little river-boat into the innermost heart of darkness. In two days' time they are eight miles from Kurtz's station, but they are forced to anchor for the night because evening is fast approaching and the river is too treacherous to navigate at night. When the morning comes, it brings with it a dense, thick, warm, clammy white fog. The "pilgrims" are completely immobilized. Then, when they hear a loud cry, first by a single voice, then by many voices, they panic. Marlowe says that the voice seemed to be that of the fog itself.

COMMENT: Perhaps in no other part of the story has Conrad so clearly insisted upon the difficulty of ascertaining reality and of delineating its antithesis—the dream. Continually, Marlowe states that the reality fades around him. At this point of suspense—we are waiting to see Kurtz, the journey is almost finished, strange sounds and sights surround the boat (a little island of civilization in the wilderness)—Conrad reveals to us that life is a process of passing between dreams and reality, and that none of us can be completely sure which is which. That life is a composite of the real and the unreal is further supported by the fact that this whole episode occurs at the physical mid-point of the story.

The "pilgrims" are afraid the natives in the jungle will attack. The cannibals who are waiting composedly aboard the river-boat signify that they are eager to confront their attackers. When Marlowe asks them why they want to fight the natives, the head cannibal replies that they want to catch them in order to "Eat 'im."

COMMENT: This brief piece of action is important for two reasons: it illustrates Conrad's idea about cannibalism which was generally accepted in his day, although it appears amusing and old-fashioned to us now; and it suggests his attitude about self-discipline. Of course, we now know that cannibalism is primarily a ritualistic activity, and has nothing at all to do with satisfying the hunger for food. Conrad, however, assumes that the cannibals enjoy human flesh, in the same way that we, for example, might be partial to pork chops. The second idea is more important: if the cannibals do enjoy human food, and we know that their own supply of food, hippo-meat, has long since gone bad, what has prevented them from devouring the "pilgrims" long ago? The only answer, according to Marlowe, must be that the cannibals have exercised a very severe kind of discipline over themselves: they have overcome their own hunger and they have subordinated that hunger to an idea. The idea may be as prosaic as "One doesn't eat one's employer," or it may be considerably more complex; but whatever it is, the cannibals respect it enough to go hungry for days. Clearly, they have a great deal of restraint and inner discipline, more than the "pilgrims" who later will shoot innocent natives merely on a whim.

Marlowe, nevertheless, believes the natives on shore will not attack, because the wailing sounds they are making are more like cries of grief than cries of warlike hostility. As it turns out, no one is completely correct. The fog lifts, and the steamer continues up the river. Only a mile and a half below their destination, they come across an island in the river. To pass by the island, it is necessary to choose a channel which takes the river-boat quite close to the shore; as a matter of fact, the boat is so close that it brushes against the bushes growing from the river bank. Then the natives attack. First, in perfect silence, thousands of arrows fly through the air, killing the poleman who operates the sounding pole. Marlowe leans over to close the shutter of the pilothouse and not ten feet away he sees the natives hidden among the bush on the shore. Marlowe's helmsman, a swaggering native, becomes hysterical and lets go of the wheel to fire a rifle into the bush. He is hit by a spear thrown from the shore, falls back into the cabin, and dies in silence in a pool of his blood. At this point Marlowe blows the river-boat's steam whistle, which terrifies the natives on shore. The shooting stops. Marlowe's shoes have become soaked in the blood of his helmsman, so he pulls them off and throws them overboard. It occurs to Marlowe that Kurtz himself must be dead.

COMMENT: Throughout this, the most action-filled scene in the story, the figure of Kurtz has been looming in the background. Before the fog has lifted, Marlowe thinks to himself that getting to Kurtz is as difficult as reaching "an enchanted princess in a fabulous castle." While still in the fog, the chief agent has authorized Marlowe to take whatever risks he wanted to reach Kurtz (although Marlowe doubts, and rightly so, his sincerity). Finally, when the helmsman's blood begins to soak into Marlowe's shoes, Marlowe is initiated into the knowledge that somehow Kurtz, too, is dead.

Marlowe is very disappointed when he believes that Kurtz must be dead. Only now does he realize how much he has been looking forward to a talk with Kurtz. As Marlowe gives way to a feeling of profound sorrow over the loss of Kurtz, he is made aware again of the sorrowing noise made by the natives in the bush. At this point there is another of those dramatic shifts, from Africa to England, as someone on the deck of the *Nellie* lets out a sigh.

> **COMMENT:** The natives, Marlowe, the listener on the deck of the *Nellie,* and possibly the reader of the story himself, all sigh for the same reason. Kurtz represents the answer to the mystery of darkness— "the illuminating . . . the pulsating stream of light . . . from the heart of an impenetrable darkness."

The omniscient (all-knowing, because he can report on everything that happens) first narrator is back with us again. Now he describes Marlowe on the deck of the *Nellie* in London, as Marlowe strikes a match to re-light his pipe. His eyelids are drooped, his face seems to recede and advance in the little light of the match until—the match goes out. Marlowe, we have been told by the narrator, has become little more than a voice. Now Marlowe, speaking of Kurtz, makes the same observation; for him, Kurtz has become little more than a voice.

> **COMMENT:** Conrad loves to introduce tiny points of light to illuminate his main characters, and then have the dimness, the obscurity, the darkness close in again. Marlowe's narrative jumps ahead in time and reveals Kurtz. After the valiant effort to reach him, Marlowe finds Kurtz has been transformed into a form of devil. Kurtz displays a rampant egoism as he refers to everything as mine—"my ivory, my station, my river." Although Marlowe recognizes that it takes some sensitivity and intellectuality for the Devil to claim someone, ordinary fools cannot be claimed, Kurtz, who "all Europe contributed to the making," has been utterly contaminated by power. Kurtz has been entrusted by the International Society for the Suppression of Savage Customs to

better the lot of the natives. Marlowe reads a report Kurtz has written for the Society. For seventeen pages the report eloquently describes how the white man can exercise powers for "good practically unbounded"; at the end, in a hand-written postscript, Kurtz has scribbled, "Exterminate all the brutes." Kurtz, for Marlowe, is dead both literally and metaphorically. Like the helmsman who died because he lacked control, he was a "tree swayed by the wind," Kurtz has capitulated to the wildnesses of the darkness. For Conrad/Marlowe, "The earth for us is a place to live in, where we must put up with sights, with sounds, with smells, too, . . . breathe dead hippo meat . . . and not be contaminated."

Marlowe sees to the burial of his helmsman in the river. He says he wants to remove temptation from the eyes of the hungry cannibal crew. Meanwhile the "pilgrims" have been discussing the probability of Kurtz's death and of the destruction of the company trading post. As they discuss plans to flee down the river, the trading post comes into view. It has not been de-stroyed. Marlowe scans the area with his glasses and notices several posts around the large shed on the summit of the hill. He assumes that these are the remains of a fence. The upper ends had been ornamented with round carved balls. Standing on the shore is a man, a European, beckoning the ship to land. The man is dressed like a harlequin in a suit that has been patched with many brightly colored pieces of cloth. Marlowe lands the river-boat and interviews the peculiarly dressed stranger. He finds that the harlequin, son of a Russian arch-priest, left the cut wood down the river, and it is he who has been reading Towson's book on navigation, *An Inquiry into Some Points of Seamanship*.

COMMENT: At this point, the end of the second section of Conrad's story, we are in the very heart of darkness itself. We can expect to reach the innermost point of the story soon, although we must remember that the first narrator has called Marlowe's tales "inconclusive." The clownishly dressed European turns out to be a Russian who believes implicitly in the great idealism of Kurtz—"this man has enlarged my mind"—and becomes interesting because he may represent for us an immature vision of life that Conrad may have shared at one stage of his development.

PART III: OUT OF THE HEART OF DARKNESS

The young motley European describes his relationship with Kurtz. It seems he has known Kurtz on and off for two years and when Kurtz fell ill it was the Russian who nursed him back to health. Marlowe hears of Kurtz's ivory raids and of his mysterious sway over the natives. "They adored him," says the Russian, for "he came to them with thunder and lightning." There was nothing to restrict Kurtz from doing whatever he pleased, even killing. Now, though, Kurtz is very ill, and the young man pleads with Marlowe to take him away quickly from the village.

> **COMMENT:** As we learn more "facts" about Kurtz, do we actually get to "know" him better? Examine how Conrad describes the relationship between the harlequin and Kurtz. "They had come together unavoidably"—why? We are never told; instead we are titillated by some curious description. They came together like two becalmed ships which "lay rubbing sides at last." They talked all night long about "Everything! Everything!" and "Of love too." But it is not love in carnal form, "It was in general." When there were ruptures in their friendship, "their *intercourse* had been very much broken." Is Conrad just flavoring his narrative or revealing some basic sexuality that permeates the relationship between the glamour-hungry youth and the all-powerful elder man? Conrad/Marlowe never tells us; neither does he explain the nature of Kurtz's influence over the natives. All we can do is speculate again about the nature of the man, Kurtz. Is he a madman? Is he a sadist? Does he really exist? Or is he imaginary—a mythic being or a character in a fable?

At the end of the Russian's narrative Marlowe looks toward the hill and the house upon it as if he needs to clarify the questions that surround Kurtz. Now he can see more clearly the posts around the house. They are not part of a fence as he had originally supposed; each post is topped by a human head. Marlowe speculates about the reasons for Kurtz's strange lusts, lusts that were aroused when he plunged into the jungle. He concludes that like the helmsman on board the river boat, Kurtz "lacked restraint." The jungle had found out that Kurtz was really "hollow at the core."

> **COMMENT:** The mystery about Kurtz is at once partially clarified and made less clear. We realize that Kurtz has indulged in "ceremonies" that would be shocking to a European. We suspect that these "ceremonies" in part help to keep the admiration of the natives. We are told that, in part, the rituals demanded that when native chiefs called on Kurtz they were made to crawl before him.
>
> Conrad was a great friend and admirer of Henry James and sent him copies of his books as they were published. They corresponded often and exchanged their theories about fiction and literary criticism; there is no doubt that they were mutually influential. In this section Conrad is being clever in the same way Henry James was clever in *The Turn of the Screw*. In his tale about the depravation of young children, James never tells us in what way the young children were depraved. Thus each of us provides from our imaginations his favorite forms of depravity when he reads the story. No doubt, that depravity we supply is in many ways more interesting to us than any James might have created for us. So, too, Conrad has left undetermined the nature of the "ceremonies" allowing our own imaginations to do that for him.

Now the "pilgrims" appear, bearing Kurtz on a stretcher. Marlowe looks through his glasses and describes him. He appears very tall, nearly seven feet, and has a bald head the color of ivory. As the "pilgrims" descend the hill there is a howl from the natives and they pour from the forest until the cleared space is filled with them. Kurtz raises himself to speak to them, and

Marlowe sees that he is nothing but skin and bones. Kurtz speaks to the natives, and they quietly disappear into the forest again. Kurtz is brought aboard the river-boat and given his letters to read. After reading one of the letters, Kurtz tells Marlowe "I am glad," signifying that Marlowe has been well spoken of by someone back in civilization. Marlowe leaves Kurtz and joins the Russian on deck and they both watch fascinatedly as a magnificent, gorgeous apparition of a woman strides beside the ship on the shore. The Russian swears he will kill her if she steps on board; he alludes to a feud with her over the colored patches he is wearing. The woman raises her arms toward the sky as if trying to touch the heavens and then slowly walks away.

> **COMMENT:** More than a touch of the absurd suffuses this series of events. Kurtz appears as if he had been "carried up from the ground." Completely naked savages immediately pour around Kurtz's stretcher. Marlowe resents the absurd danger of the situation hoping that "the man who can talk so well of love in general will find some particular reason to spare us this time." His name, Kurtz,—which means "short" in German—belies Kurtz's actual height and was "as true as everything else in his life—and death." The sick man appears as a phantom, more dead than alive, but when he opens his mouth, he appears as if he wants to swallow everything. The magnificent, opulently dressed goddess has squabbled over some measly shreds and patches of clothing. Remembering that this is the first time we encounter Kurtz in the flesh, or lack of it, it is entirely appropriate that Conrad should draw upon a wealth of grotesquerie to underpin our first encounter with the specter. Kurtz is too heightened a reality to be confronted plainly without the cover of extraordinary event.

The manager and Kurtz have an argument in Kurtz's cabin. Kurtz points out that it is the ivory, not Kurtz, that the manager is interested in saving and vows that he will return to carry out his ideas. The manager leaves the cabin and realizes that Marlowe has overheard the argument. He claims that Kurtz is very sick, by way of excusing the shouted accusations. Further, the manager complains that Kurtz had ruined the district for ivory trading and that his methods are "unsound." Marlowe is utterly disgusted and tells us that he identifies with Kurtz in the face of this vile alternative. He is glad, at any rate, to have a "choice of nightmares."

> **COMMENT**: Marlowe, as we recall, has been looking forward to meeting Kurtz throughout the voyage; his first reaction at seeing Kurtz's unspeakable practices, however, is one of abhorrence. When Marlowe hears that the manager decries the "ceremonies" because they hamper efficient trading he is disgusted all over again. Faced with the nightmare of debased idealism on the one hand and the nightmare of empty efficiency on the other, he will choose the God gone wrong because it connotes a sort of tortured heroism. It remains to be seen if Marlowe will survive his impulsive identification with the depraved nightmare.

Now the Russian enters to expand the information he has been giving about Kurtz. It seems that it was Kurtz himself who ordered the attack upon the steamboat and he worries that Kurtz's reputation might be damaged as a result. After borrowing a pair of shoes, "good English tobacco," and some rifle shells, he departs from the ship and reenters the jungle. Marlowe awakes at midnight to discover that Kurtz has disappeared. He experiences a deep "moral shock" but he does not give the alarm (Marlowe says that he must be true to his choice of nightmare). He immediately sets out in pursuit of the "shadow." He feels intensely possessive about this search but cannot understand why he doesn't want to share this experience with anyone. On the bank of the river he finds a broad trail through the grass; Kurtz, too weak to walk, has crawled "on all-fours," and Marlowe imagines that he will beat Kurtz if he catches him. He knows that he wants to prevent Kurtz from reaching the natives who are gathered around large fires in the jungle. At this point Marlowe has a fantasy of the old knitting woman being at the end of the path.

> **COMMENT**: One way of interpreting the action of the story

is to see it as a descent into Hell, an idea used in such classical epics as the *Odyssey* and the *Aeneid*. If we read the story in this way, then those knitting women back in Brussels can be interpreted as the Fates, who spin, measure, and cut the thread of life. Who then would be a more appropriate figure to find at the end of that jungle trail, practically in the very center of the heart of darkness, than she who measures off our lives, and ends them?

This descent can also be seen as a descent into a psychological hell. Kurtz, regressing psychologically, is so emotionally sick that he must proceed like a crawling baby— he has lost his manly stature. Marlowe has begun to regress too: he feels an urge to beat up Kurtz, he sees the old woman /mother figure, he then notices the pilgrims "squirting lead out of Winchesters held to the hip." Finally, Marlowe has begun to lose his identity as a civilized man and starts to identify his heartbeat with the beating of the jungle drums.

Marlowe manages to circle around ahead of Kurtz as "though it had been a boyish game." Still, when he confronts Kurtz, they are only a few feet from the nearest fire and Kurtz has but to raise his voice to summon the natives. Marlowe tries to reason with Kurtz, telling him he will be "utterly lost" if he refuses to return to the river-boat. Kurtz replies that he was on the verge of "immense plans" which will be spoiled. Of the ensuing argument, Marlowe says that Kurtz himself was rational, but it was his soul that was mad. Marlowe wins and half carries Kurtz, who "was not much heavier than a child," back to the river-boat. The next day they leave on the trip back down the river.

COMMENT: Here is the climax of the story: we cannot go forward and we cannot go back without something of the most consequential nature happening. Marlowe must leave the track, that is, leave conventional paths to discover the dark truths of Kurtz's condition. And these truths hover around the central question of identity—who are we? It is only when Marlowe holds up the lost image of Kurtz for

Kurtz to see, that he can be persuasive. Marlowe sees the problem as that of identifying Kurtz with his civilized personality and breaking the spell of the wilderness "that seemed to draw him to its pitiless breast by the awakening of forgotten and brutal instincts." A corollary of Marlowe's insight is that he too must "go through the ordeal of looking into myself." Kurtz's 'lostness' is really a metaphor for the alienation we all must face.

The river-boat leaves amid violence and murder. As it swings around in the river, the natives gather on the shore. In the front are three medicine men, horned and stained, periodically shouting words that do not resemble human language. The beautiful woman with the "helmeted head and tawny cheeks" rushes out to the very brink of the stream. Marlowe sees the "pilgrims" on the deck of the river-boat preparing to fire upon the unsuspecting natives, so he blows the steam whistle again and again until the frightened natives run from the terrifying sound. Only the majestic woman remains unmoved by the screeching whistle. At this point the "pilgrims" open fire on the natives. Kurtz has been moved to the pilot house, so he and Marlowe have the opportunity for long talks as they travel down the river. Kurtz tells Marlowe of his grandiose plans for the future and of the girl he wishes to marry, his "Intended." One evening, as the boat is stopped for repairs, Kurtz loses confidence in his chances for recovery and tells Marlowe that he will die. Marlowe tries to comfort him, but suddenly Kurtz changes his expression, as if he had a glimpse into "complete knowledge." Kurtz cries, "The horror! The horror!" Later that evening the manager's servant boy contemptuously announces, "Mistah Kurtz—he dead."

COMMENT: These are perhaps the most famous of Conrad's words: "The horror! The horror!" and "Mistah Kurtz —he dead." T. S. Eliot, in his poem *The Hollow Men,* uses the latter as an epigraph. Of course, the arguments of the critics have been hot and furious over what Kurtz meant. However, isn't it a mark of Conrad's artistry that he could introduce his ambiguity at so crucial a moment in the story, and demand of the reader that he supply the "horror" just as earlier he demanded that the reader supply the concrete detail for those "ceremonies"? Whatever the real nature of the "horror," it shows us that Kurtz died in torment, both disappointed in his failure to accomplish his goals, and perhaps horrified by the savagery implicit in those goals.

The "pilgrims" buried Kurtz and Marlowe's next words are that they very nearly buried him. Marlowe himself falls deathly ill after Kurtz dies and describes his battle for life as being fought "in a sickly atmosphere of tepid scepticism, without much belief in your right and still less in that of your adversary." Still shaky spiritually, Marlowe finds himself back in the "sepulchral city," where he resents the petty, illusion-ridden people scurrying about flaunting "folly in the face of a danger it is unable to comprehend." Several visitors interested in Kurtz ply Marlowe for information.

During conversations with a cousin and a journalist Marlowe discovers that Kurtz had enormous capabilities as a musician and as a political leader—"he could get himself to believe anything." Tearing off the postscript, Marlowe hands the journalist Kurtz's report. Finally, Marlowe is left with a packet of Kurtz's letters written to his "Intended." He visits Kurtz's fiancee nearly a year after the events on the river. He finds her dressed in black, so that her white face seems to float in the air. He finds her still devoted to the illusion that Kurtz was a great man devoted to the ideal of doing good. When she questions Marlowe about Kurtz's last words, Marlowe cannot bring himself to tell the truth and he lies, telling her that his last words were of her. Again we flash, for the last time, back to the deck of the *Nellie,* and the story concludes with Marlowe sitting silently, "In the pose of a meditating Buddha."

COMMENT: The puzzle of Kurtz has still not been solved. To the last Marlowe continues to discover facets of his personality and we are never able to define Kurtz once and for all. Somehow he floats above and beyond us, searching vaingloriously but searching nevertheless; the first narrator has been true to his words: Marlowe has told one of his "inconclusive" tales. Nevertheless, Kurtz remains for many writers after Conrad, the prototype of twentieth-century man, tragically divided against himself.،

Although sensitive people can and are affected by the literary experience, Conrad was too shrewd to overlook the fact that most people lack the training and/or the insight to understand what life is all about. Despite Kurtz's thoroughgoing falsity, he is still regarded by Conrad/Marlowe as a victor because he has the one clear moment before he dies—the moment of disillusionment. He is able, in short, to see into himself. The others on board the *Nellie,* with the exception of the narrator, are profoundly unimpressed by Marlowe's experience. All they can do is regret that as a result of listening to such a long story they "have lost the first of the ebb." Perhaps Conrad is saying that Marlowe's tales are inconclusive because his listeners are such inconclusive listeners, more attuned to a physical tide than to the spiritual ebb and flow in humanity.

CHARACTER ANALYSES

THE NARRATOR: He is the fifth man "present" on board the *Nellie*. As a result of listening to Marlowe's story he undergoes a moral transformation. As Seymour Gross has pointed out, the narrator perceives optimistically at the beginning of the tale: the Thames is flooded in a "benign immensity of unstained light." At the end the narrator, like Marlowe, understands some of the brute realities inherent in life and the Thames "seemed to lead into the heart of an immense darkness." By a kind of rhetorical trick the narrator merges in function with the reader and he doesn't so much relate the story as he is converted by it. Unlike the others who disregard the tale as absurd, the narrator achieves precisely what Marlowe achieved—"some knowledge of yourself."

CHARLES MARLOWE: Superficially he is a man of action, a sailor very interested in "doing his job well." He also understands that sticking to the track means more than giving the appearance of fidelity. This story can be read as a tale of the staggering implications of going off the track and of Marlowe's discovery of his own capabilities for "losing the way."

MR. KURTZ: The superlative product of Western European civilization, he enters the wilderness with the progressive idea of uplifting the savages. He has not prepared himself inwardly for the primitive assault the jungle can encourage, so he responds to it with an unsuspected primitivism of his own. Although he is "hollow at the core," he is able to estimate truly the emptiness of his existence. "The horror! The horror!" is his dying summation of what he has become and what he might have been. His self-divided agony and his moral collapse are thematic concerns which occupy a great deal of modern literature.

THE MANAGER: As company manager in the central station he has somehow "managed" to survive the oppressions of the jungle. In spite of the fact that he is painted as an essentially hollow man, he is jealous of Kurtz's success and very suspicious of his humanitarianism. His machine-like personality is a counterpoint for the wild idealism of Kurtz and for Marlowe is a poorer "choice of nightmare."

THE BRICKMAKER: A man entirely capable of living a pointless existence—there is not a brick at the station for him to work with—he conspires with the manager against Kurtz. Another empty man, he is described accurately—a "papier-mâché Mephistopheles."

THE PILGRIMS: Avaricious employees of the company, they anonymously make their mock pilgrimage to the interior for the sole purpose of exploitation. Capable of murder, they are awful perversions of the colonial spirit. These depersonalized 'furies' have even been referred to as the 'black man's burden.'

THE MANAGER'S UNCLE: Aptly described as "a butcher in a

poor neighborhood," he leads the Eldorado Expedition in search of plunder.

THE MANAGER'S BOY: As if to show that chattel takes on the character of the owner, this "overfed young Negro from the coast" is shrewish and insolent. It is he who announces contemptuously that Kurtz is dead. It is characteristic of Conrad's narrative artistry to make so minor a personage deliver such important information. We are surprised by the sudden flatness of the news—"Mistah Kurtz—he dead," but it is an altogether fitting termination to an illusion-ridden life.

THE HARLEQUIN: Another improbable character, he gives Marlowe two kinds of information about Kurtz. He relates Kurtz's external activities in the jungle and, also, by describing Kurtz's influence over him, he provides additional insight into Kurtz's inner power. Deliberately conceived as a clownish romantic, the harlequin is an ideal convert to Kurtz's doomed illusions. Aside from his narrative function of moving Marlowe closer to the inner station, the young Russian may also serve as a bizarre embodiment of the innocent adventurer who is willing to risk everything because he hasn't the vaguest idea of the costs involved. Marlowe recognizes the flimsy character of the harlequin when he describes him as wearing "pretty rags—rags that would fly off at the first good shake." By contrasting the insubstantiality of the harlequin with the solid searching of Marlowe, we are disabused of the notion that Marlowe is simply glamour-hungry.

KURTZ'S JUNGLE MISTRESS: Bordering on the surreal, she appears whenever Kurtz is in danger of abandoning her. Conrad never fills in the relation between Kurtz and the savage woman, but spares no detail when he describes her fantastic and rich clothing. More statue than woman, she is thoroughly devoted to her "White God."

MY INTENDED: The civilized antithesis to the savage woman, she is ironically dressed in mourning clothes when Marlowe confronts her. Marlowe decides against telling her the truth about

Kurtz's last words; the illusion of Kurtz will sustain her even from the grave.

MARLOWE'S AUNT: She is instrumental in giving Marlowe the opportunity of voyaging into the heart of darkness. She is representative of all women who, because they are "out of touch with the truth," must be kept from the truth.

THE HELMSMAN: A swaggering, boastful man who panics as he steers the river-boat. Marlowe's shoes fill with the dying helmsman's blood thus symbolizing a kinship between Marlowe, who is preparing to leave the 'track' and one who already has.

THE CANNIBALS: The primitive crew of Marlowe's ship who exhibit more self-restraint than the civilized "pilgrims." Even though they are starving, they refuse to eat their masters, exhibiting to Marlowe a kind of "primitive honour."

THE KNITTING WOMEN: Symbolic guardians of the door of darkness, they act as company representatives mysteriously endowed with the knowledge of fatefulness. Their mundane activity belies their Cassandra-like function.

THE COMPANY DOCTOR: Along with the knitters, this professional dramatically foreshadows the threat of the heart of darkness. He measures the skull of Marlowe but is more interested in what's going to happen inside his head.

THE ACCOUNTANT: Marlowe admires this man for doing his job properly and keeping his books in "apple-pie order." He is one of the few company administrators who commands Marlowe's respect.

FRESLEVEN: The ex-river-boat captain is replaced by Marlowe. He has sadistically attacked an old Negro and has been killed by a tribal chieftain's son. He represents for Marlowe the bizarre effects the jungle can have on sanity.

THE SWEDISH CAPTAIN: Marlowe travels in the captain's steamer to the first company station. The captain indicates that strange things happen to people who go up the river.

THE COMPANY REPRESENTATIVE: He is a final emissary of company greed, determined to retrieve Kurt's writings in the hope they will contain valuable geographical information about the jungle territory.

KURTZ'S COUSIN: He talks with Marlowe about Kurtz's vast musical ability.

THE JOURNALIST: He tells Marlowe that Kurtz had unlimited political capabilities because of his forensic powers.

THE SECRET SHARER

INTRODUCTION

Like *Heart of Darkness* and *Lord Jim* before it, *The Secret Sharer* is one of Conrad's most personal tales, taking incidents, characters, and even ships out of Conrad's seafaring years. Although *The Secret Sharer* was written ten years after *Lord Jim,* there is biographical evidence to show that Conrad actually was brought back in his thinking to the period from which *Lord Jim* was drawn. Conrad's biographer, Gerard Jean-Aubry, and one of his most sensitive critics, Albert Guerard, tell the story of how *The Secret Sharer* was written.

In 1909, Conrad was working on *Under Western Eyes.* He received a visit from a Captain Morris, a man who still sailed Eastern seas as Conrad had in his earlier years. Apparently the visit caused Conrad to remember the East very vividly, because he wrote to a friend: "I had a visit from a man out of the Malay Seas. It was like the raising of a lot of dead. . . ." Conrad dropped *Under Western Eyes,* and in two weeks in November wrote *The Secret Sharer.*

If we move back to Conrad's seafaring days we can pick up the rest of the evidence for a parallel relationship between the creation of *Lord Jim* and *The Secret Sharer.* In the summer of 1880, two events shocked the sailors in the East. One event was the *Jeddah* affair, which Conrad used in *Lord Jim* as a model for the *Patna* affair. The other scandal involved the *Cutty Sark,* a famous American clipper ship. (This same ship, by the way, figures in Hart Crane's poem *The Bridge*.) A mate aboard the *Cutty Sark* killed one of the crew in a fit of anger. The captain, Captain Wallace, took pity on the mate. Instead of bringing him to trial for the murder, Wallace allowed him to escape to another ship. Four days later, Captain Wallace committed suicide as he jumped off his ship into shark-infested waters. This evidence, ably documented in *A Hell-Ship Voyage* by Basil Lubbock, in addition to such internal evidence as similarity of theme and narrator, causes most critics to connect *Lord Jim, Heart of Darkness,* and *The Secret Sharer*. Other critics insist upon the identification of *The Shadow Line* as a brother or twin to *The Secret Sharer*.

Despite all the factual data which points to his own adventures as the source of Conrad's fictive adventures, history in the hands of an artist is different from history in the textbook. In the *Poetics,* Aristotle differentiated the tasks of poetry and history:

> Poetry, therefore, is a more philosophical and a higher thing than history: for poetry tends to express the universal, history the particular. By the universal I mean how a person of a certain type will on occasion speak or act, according to the law of probability or necessity; and it is this universality at which poetry aims in the names she attaches to the personages. The particular is—for example—what Alcibiades did or suffered.

Conrad believed implicitly in the Aristotelian definition of the role of a poet. Conrad declared that he created character for the purpose of revealing information about us all and not just for the purposes of a particular illumination: fiction approaches art, he said, "the more it acquires a symbolic character. . . . All the great creations of literature have been symbolic, and in that way have gained in complexity, in power, in depth and in beauty." It is wise when dealing with Conrad's stories to follow the dictum of D. H. Lawrence: "Never trust the artist. Trust the tale."

THE NARRATIVE TECHNIQUE OF THE SECRET SHARER: Unlike *Heart of Darkness,* Conrad dispenses with his technique of interrupted narrative and multiple persons telling the story. There is no tonal differentiating between divergent narrators and no skipping back and forth in time. One is struck immediately by the smooth flow of the narration. *The Secret Sharer* uses only one first-person narrator, the Captain, who remains unnamed, although he may be a younger Marlowe. No omniscient narrator is necessary: the first words belong to the young captain himself. Conrad employs only one flashback, Leggatt's story. Of course, the plot line of *The Secret Sharer* is much simpler than that of *Heart of Darkness* and as a result Conrad has more room, aesthetically, to present the psychological and moral dilemmas of his main characters.

PLOT ANALYSIS

CHAPTER I

As the story opens, the young Captain is standing on the deck of his ship, his first command. The ship itself is anchored at the mouth of the Meinam River, at the head of the Gulf of Siam. The Captain is about to take his ship back home to England, as soon as he has a favorable wind. In the meantime, he surveys the scene and describes it.

The shoreline is extremely flat, so that the land and the sea seem to be two parts of the same surface, but of different colors. The Meinam River follows a serpentine course on its way to the sea. As the tugboat which had brought the ship out from land disappears from the Captain's view, he watches the trail of its smoke up the river. To his left the Captain notices a line of small islands "suggesting ruins of stone walls, towers, and block-houses," and to his right lines of "half-submerged" fishing stakes. As the sun sets the ship's spars cast long shadows to the east. In the fading light, the Captain notices the masts of another ship on the other side of the line of islands. His "quiet communion" with his ship is broken by sounds of activity on the ship.

> **COMMENT:** The key passage in this section reads: "In this breathless pause at the threshold of a long passage we seemed to be measuring our fitness for a long and arduous enterprise, the appointed task of both our existences to be carried out, far from all human eyes, with only sky and sea for spectators and for judges." Obviously the captain is preparing for something more than a physical ordeal; the religious silence

of communion permeates the atmosphere. A pagoda looms above the monotonously flat land, the incense-like smoke of the departing tug and the shadows of the spars cloud the earthly physicality of the Captain's view. He intends to accomplish something "far from all human eyes."

Sitting down to supper with his two officers, we learn some of the Captain's problems: he is unfamiliar with his ship and his officers; he is worried that his officers won't respect him; and most important, the Captain confesses, "I was somewhat of a stranger to myself."

COMMENT: He wonders "how far I should turn out faithful to that ideal conception of one's own personality every man sets up for himself secretly." With this statement in mind the journey can be interpreted on two levels. On the first level, the journey is the vehicle for an adventure story in which the Captain helps Leggatt escape from the law. On a second level, the journey is the means by which the Captain discovers himself.

Karen Horney, a modern psychologist, has posited that in order to resolve neurotic conflicts within the self, men create idealizations: images which propel men to fulfill goals of glory. These images are accompanied by an image of self-rejection in which the individual perceives of himself as despicable and unloved. Neither is true to the real self which strives to emerge to a middle ground. If, as most critics tend to believe, the Captain's idealization is not the product of neurotic conflict, why then should it be "secret"? Why should ideality be embarrassing to him? This does not mean to indicate that Conrad's heroes are all neurotically driven, yet in view of Kurtz and *his* illusion, we must consider the possibility that all of Conrad's figures may be psychologically defective—as, possibly, we all are.

During supper the second mate divulges information about the anchored ship. It is the *Sephora,* a Liverpool ship carrying a load of coal and bound for Bangkok. After dinner the Captain surprises his officers by announcing that he himself will stand watch that night; he wants to give the crew a rest. Thus the Captain is again alone on the deck of the ship as night falls. For a second time, we have a careful, precise description of the scene.

The ship is cleared for sea; she is "roomy" for her size, and she is "very inviting." In the rigging, a riding light is burning, "with a clear, untroubled, as if symbolic flame. . . ." The Captain, barefooted, is smoking a cigar; it, too, burns with a singular light. On his tour of the ship, the Captain notices that a rope ladder has been left hanging over the side. He becomes annoyed because, "exactitude in small matters is the very soul of discipline." Reflecting further, the Captain realizes that if he had not given the crew the night off, the ladder would have been stowed. By interfering with the routine of the ship, he has caused a breach of discipline. He asks himself "whether it was wise ever to interfere with the established routine of duties even from the kindest motives."

COMMENT: This piece of action artfully foreshadows the central moral problem of *The Secret Sharer*—how does one reconcile the demands of the society with personal, humanitarian imperatives? As the story unfolds, the Captain will protect Leggatt from the law because of his sympathy for him as a human being. As if pointing this out to us symbolically, Conrad spotlights his theme with the "riding light" and the Captain's cigar—the beacon of society vs. one's personal light of responsibility.

The Captain grabs the rope ladder to draw it up, but there is an unaccountable resistance; he leans over the ship's rail and sees a shocking sight—the naked, headless body of a man floating alongside the ship. The cigar drops from the Captain's mouth and lands with a hiss in the water below. In the next instant, the swimmer below (for he is a swimmer, not a corpse; his head was made invisible in the night because his hair is black) raises his face to look up. The swimmer very calmly asks for the skipper of the ship and when the Captain tells him who he is, the swimmer introduces himself as Leggatt and comes aboard.

COMMENT: As the title of this story would indicate, Leggatt shares a secret with the Captain. His name, a homonym for "legate," means an emissary or ambassador. But where does he originate and what does he share with the Captain? One theory based on this early description of Leggatt assumes Leggatt to be the unconscious primitive id of the Captain. We notice that the Captain's head, leaning over the side of the ship, completes the "headless" body of the swimmer below. Leggatt arises fishlike from the sea paralleling the emergence of the foetus from the amniotic fluid. The swimmer is so self-possessed that he does not even ask permission to board, as if to indicate that he belongs with the Captain. Of course Conrad is not one to state the relationship baldly; he will insist on the "mysterious communication" between them. Conrad prefers a broader statement of their relationship; the following can mean almost anything: "The self-possession of that man had somehow induced a corresponding state in myself." "Self-possession" may be taken both literally and figuratively which is why Conrad, although a great intuitive psychologist, primarily functions as a literary craftsman.

After Leggatt comes aboard, the Captain gets him a suit of pajamas ("sleeping suit") to wear, the same kind that the Captain himself wears. Standing together on the aft deck, "barefooted," Leggatt tells his story. He was mate on the *Sephora* when she was caught in a fierce storm at sea. The Captain became so frightened by the tempest that he was incapable of giving orders himself; Leggatt took command of the ship and gave the order that saved the ship from certain destruction: reef the foresail. Leggatt himself went forward to help the sailors with their difficult task. As he was directing the crew, one of them refused to carry out his orders and defied Leggatt. In the heat of the moment, Leggatt knocked the man to the deck causing the crewman to leap for Leggatt's throat. As the two men struggled, a huge wave buried the ship; when the deck was cleared, the crew found Leggatt wedged in a corner, his hands still closed around the throat of the rebellious member of the crew, who was dead. The crew cried out, "Murder!" Leggatt was arrested and locked in his cabin for the remainder of the voyage.

> **COMMENT:** Even though Leggatt has told his story directly enough, certain ambiguities persist. His crime, if that is what it was, is questionable from several viewpoints. Did Leggatt actually kill the rebellious crewman, or was the man drowned by the huge wave? If Leggatt did strangle the man, was his crime justifiable homicide? Furthermore, Leggatt is no "homicidal ruffian" and the dead man was "one of those miserable devils that have no business to live at all."
>
> Twice during his narrative Leggatt recalls that "My father's a parson in Norfolk," and twice he wonders how a respectable jury and judge would react to his "sufficiently fierce story." Conrad seems to be balancing questions of personal guilt against society's tendencies to indict and prejudge.

After listening to the first part of Leggatt's story the Captain secretes Leggatt within his own stateroom, a room so shaped as to afford privacy even with the door open. Safely hidden, Leggatt rests by the porthole and continues his story. He had asked the captain of the *Sephora* to let him escape. Fearful of what his wife and steward might say, the captain refused. Later on, taking advantage of an unlocked cabin door, Leggatt made a dash for the rail and jumped overboard before anyone could stop him. Under cover of the night, he swam to a small barren islet. Realizing he couldn't survive there, he disrobed completely and swam out for the riding light of the Captain's ship. When he reached the ship's ladder he was completely exhausted. The Captain helps him into his bed and then remarks, "he must have looked exactly as I used to look in that bed."

> **COMMENT:** Leggatt introduces an interesting motif when he

compares his crime to "The 'brand of Cain' business." He recognizes that he may have violated a primal moral law, but in the next breath he says that "I was ready enough to go off wandering on the face of the earth—and that was price enough to pay for an Abel of that sort." Leggatt somehow has managed to come to terms with himself; Conrad presents him as a man who has learned to live with his "superego." Leggatt refuses to live in the shadow of societal demands; his sense of self is too strong—the role of "outcast" intimidates him not one bit. Perhaps the Captain notices Leggatt's innate strength when he remarks, "He was not a bit like me, really."

The Captain and Leggatt work out elaborate precautions so that Leggatt will not be discovered by the rest of the crew. The biggest problem is to conceal Leggatt when the steward cleans the Captain's cabin every morning. One device they develop is to have the Captain take a bath while the steward is busy in the cabin, and to have Leggatt stand in a corner of the bathroom out of sight. They successfully dupe the steward when they have to face a new crisis: the skipper of the *Sephora* has pulled alongside looking for Leggatt.

COMMENT: One wonders at the annoyingly repetitive references to Leggatt as the Captain's "second self." Over and over again the Captain refers to him as "the secret sharer of my life," "my double," "identical attitudes," "as though I had been faced by my own reflection in the depths of a somber and immense mirror." Marvin Murdick claims that these references so vulgarize the story as to make it cheap clinical psychology. Yet, if we interpret this tale as more than simply an adventure story of escape and rescue and invest it with psychological and symbolic meanings, perhaps Leggatt doesn't really exist except in the Captain's mind and the insistent and annoying references may be the insistent and annoying echoes that are seemly in a divided psyche.

For Murdick a much more artistically penetrating symbol

is the L-shaped room which diagrams both the allegory of the Captain's divided soul and the allegory of the artist's split soul. Henry James seems to substantiate the idea that an artist is advised to use his symbols sparingly; there is an "odd law by which the minimum of valid suggestion always serves the man of imagination better than the maximum," he once said.

However, one wonders if the efficiency of any one symbol in a story isn't dependent on the play around each other symbol. That is, if the image of the double weren't so over-used, would the L-shaped room be as telling? Near the end of the chapter the Captain describes the "dual working" of his mind and he discovers, "It was very much like being mad, only it was worse, because one was aware of it." If Conrad deleted most of the symbolized references to his double image, would the above apprehension have been as revealingly poignant? It seems that Conrad's artistry demands that we accept even his thrilled insistencies if we are to accept his giant insistency—the story itself.

CHAPTER II

Captain Archbold, the captain of the *Sephora* comes on deck and meets with the Captain. They go below, into the very state-room where Leggatt is hiding. Feigning defective hearing, the Captain forces Archbold to relate the tale of the murder loud enough so that Leggatt can overhear. According to Archbold there is no doubt that Leggatt killed the mutinous seaman. However, when we learn that Captain Archbold believes he himself gave the order to reef the foresail, we begin to doubt his words entirely. As the conversation draws to a close we discover that the Captain is particularly anxious that Archbold not ask about the whereabouts of Leggatt directly; it seems that the Captain is incapable of uttering a direct lie. This is explained as being predicated on "psychological (not moral) reasons."

COMMENT: We have some clear evidence here that the Captain bears more than a passing relation to the character of Marlowe. We remember in *Heart of Darkness* that Marlowe confessed there was nothing he hated so much as a lie. We also remember that as the Captain verges on lying when Archbold leaves, claiming the "privilege of defective hearing," Marlowe actually lied to Kurtz's "Intended" when she asked to know Kurtz's last words.

Archbold, as his name indicates, possesses a cloying strength. He embodies conventional wisdom in his "spiritless tenacity." It is he who whimpers during the storm, not Leggatt. Plainly antithetical to spirited Leggatt, he admits that he never liked him—Leggatt was too smart, too gentlemanly to suit his plain tastes. Operating under an obscure, incomprehensible tenacity, Archbold is "under some pitiless obligation" to bring Leggatt to justice. The heartlessness of habit and the entrapments of society (isn't his wife aboard?) have vanquished the Captain of the *Sephora;* he rules but does not command.

After Captain Archbold leaves, a slight wind comes up allowing the ship to get under way. The Captain continues his efforts to secrete Leggatt and seems to be cracking under the constant strain. One day he spots his steward moving toward his cabin with a jacket of his that has been wet by a passing shower. In order to alert Leggatt he fairly shouts out the steward's name. Finally, after the ship has been under way for a few days, Leggatt and the Captain agree that Leggatt must be put ashore before he is discovered by the crew, who are becoming suspicious of the Captain's bizarre behavior.

COMMENT: The problem of hiding Leggatt is compounded by the problem the Captain faced when he assumed command: how to confidently master a ship. He notices how irresolute he is when he issues orders—"There are to a seaman certain words, gestures, that should in given conditions come as naturally, as instinctively as the winking of a menaced eye . . . But all unconscious alertness had abandoned me." Conrad is indicating that self-mastery is a function of the inner as well as the outer environment. The

Captain complains that when he goes on deck he leaves part of himself below in his cabin; he feels that he is in two places at once. The confusion within the Captain mounts until he begins to speak in conspiratorial whispers to his first mate.

The ship is sailing in the middle of the Gulf of Siam. The Captain decides to land Leggatt on the island of Koh-ring since it looks like it is capable of supporting life. The plan is to steer the ship as close to shore as possible, to turn it about, and to have Leggatt dive overboard as the ship turns. Leggatt is a strong swimmer, so he should easily make the shore, ready to start a new life.

COMMENT: When the Captain reveals his plan for sailing dangerously close to the land, the crew is astounded. It is interesting that although the Captain's plan to move through uncharted and dangerous reefs at night is patently absurd, not one crew member voices his disapproval. Whereas Leggatt broke with the conventions of the sea in order to save the *Sephora,* no one can break the conventions aboard the Captain's ship, not even the first mate who has said that he likes to account for everything. There is a subtle paralleling of crisis situations between the *Sephora* in the midst of storm and the Captain's ship as it heads landward.

That night, the plan of escape is put into operation. Leggatt takes up a position in the sail locker, from which he will dive when the ship turns. Just as he says good-by to Leggatt, the Captain impulsively gives Leggatt the floppy hat he had been wearing all day. Determined to give Leggatt every possible advantage, the Captain decides it is "a matter of conscience to shave the land as close as possible." As the ship drives closer and closer to the land, the crew grows uneasy. Finally, even the Captain is frightened. He tells us that he dared not look, the ship was so close to shore. When it is within the very shadow of the land itself, the crew cry out in terror: the ship is lost; they will surely crash upon the shore. Now the Captain gives the order, "Hard alee!" The shadow of the land casts such a pall over the ship, that it is impossible for the Captain to see whether or not his ship is coming about. At that instant he looks down in the water and sees a "white object floating within a yard of the ship's side . . . my own floppy hat." The hat serves the Captain as a marker, and he can successfully maneuver the ship out to the open sea. He leaves Leggatt behind, swimming for the shore, "a free man, a proud swimmer, striking out for a new destiny."

COMMENT: A posssible interpretation of the concluding section could derive from the findings of depth psychology. Having explored Leggatt, really his own subconscious mind, the Captain now is free himself to go forward into life, secure in the knowledge of himself and of his ship. He has been freed from the burden of guilts and violent drives. The hat, in Jungian terms, is a symbol of the integrity of the self. In releasing the hat to Leggatt, the Captain is truly giving of himself. When Leggatt allows the hat to drift away, he is releasing his hold over the Captain. It is, then, the Captain who really strikes out for a new destiny. Another, less psychological, interpretation of the meaning of the hat is to regard it as a symbol of illusion. The hat symbolizes the Captain's "sudden pity for his mere flesh. It had been meant to save his homeless head from the danger of the sun." Its purpose was to protect Leggatt from the searing rays of truth. But what truth? Leggatt had rationalized his killing of the man by saying that the mutineer was really unworthy to live. By setting himself up as sort of a superman, Leggatt held himself aloof from the insane pressures of life. The Captain senses his illusion of superiority and purposely brings the ship as close as possible to the shore to show Leggatt that one can court death without sacrificing sane regard for one's fellow man. The Captain, like the Captain aboard the *Sephora,* is terrified of the dangers of shipwreck, yet unlike Leggatt he does not strangle his mate at the moment of crisis. He shakes him violently but does not go further. The hat serves to disrupt Leggatt's version of superiority and because he can no longer abide protection from the truth, he leaves it floating behind striking out for an illusionless destiny. For the Captain the hat no longer is viable cover against reality. He has chosen "the untempted life," "the great security of the sea," but mere habit of command is insufficient knowledge for him to continue living. The Captain pursues his double because he must find in himself that sanctity of self-assurance and self-esteem that will be a true moral foundation. When he sees the floating hat he says, "I hardly thought of my other self, . . . I had what I wanted—the saving mark for my eyes." The Captain has survived the ordeal and has discovered his integrated selfhood. He too leaves the floppy white hat of illusion behind.

CHARACTER ANALYSES

THE CAPTAIN: The only narrator of *The Secret Sharer*, he presents himself at the outset as an insecure young man about to command his first voyage at sea. Becalmed, as is his ship, he needs to test himself in order to gain inner balance. He is put to the test as he tries to shield Leggatt from the iron framework of fact. When he recognizes in Leggatt his own duped superiority and submits himself to his fate (when he takes his ship into dangerous intimacy with land, fact), he is a candidate for emergence. His ideal image has been rectified and adjusted to reality.

LEGGATT: The Captain's spiritual twin, he is running away from the consequences of a homicidal act he has committed on board the *Sephora*. A well-bred, handsome young man, he believes entirely too much in his innate superiority. As a result of the unqualified support and protection he receives from the

Captain, he is brought back from his vainglorious image of himself to a sounder self-concept. It remains to be seen if he will be worthy of complete redemption. Although still contemptuous of 'Abel,' he perceives his 'Cainhood'—he understands the basic ties that bind him with the rest of humanity.

THE CHIEF MATE: A bewhiskered, totally unimaginative mariner, he likes to account for everything in his environment except himself. He functions like a disembodied intelligence who, like the scorpion who crawls into his cabin, is too close to the ground to see anything. Potentially noxious, he crumbles from fear as the Captain brings his ship close to shore.

THE SECOND MATE: Although younger than the Captain, he holds the Captain in contempt. Perennially sneering, he contributes to the atmosphere of distrust that confronts the Captain upon his first assumption of command.

THE STEWARD: In spite of the fact that the narrator calls him "harmless," he presents the most immediate threat to exposing Leggatt. When he is about to enter the cabin where Leggatt is hiding, the Captain shouts to warn Leggatt of his approach. A typically Conradian grace note, the man most colorlessly described presages the most severe consequences.

CAPTAIN ARCHBOLD: No self-doubt disturbs this man since he probably has no self to doubt—his life at sea has been too immaculate. He symbolizes what the Captain could have become if Leggatt had not come aboard.

CRITICAL COMMENTARY

Literary critics are almost unanimous in hailing Conrad as a master novelist and stylist. There are those, however, who are bothered by certain facets of Conrad's style and tend to emphasize the strength of his moral attitudes. This school, led by the British critic, F. R. Leavis, believes that Conrad follows the great tradition of English novelists, from Austen to Eliot to Dickens, who are able to dramatize the great moral and ethical issues that face society. Leavis does not particularly enjoy the adjectival excesses of Conrad's style and thinks that Conrad is on surer aesthetic grounds when he is presenting objective incident, e.g., heads on posts, to charge the atmosphere of his stories with the fantasy of truth.

CONRAD'S THEMES: In his 'Familiar Preface' to *A Personal Record,* Conrad has offered a statement which has often been taken as the summation of his thematic intentions. In it Conrad says, "Those who read me know my conviction that the world, the temporal world, rests on few simple ideas: so simple that they must be old as the hills. It rests, notable, among others, on the idea of Fidelity."

Critics have variously interpreted the meanings of "Fidelity." Douglas Hewitt notes that to read this pronouncement as a simple straightforward belief in "doing one's job" would be to miss the basic pessimism with which Conrad viewed humanity. Hewitt charges Conrad with a form of "nihilism"—believing that his characters face their problems against a background which cannot be changed and which ultimately must defeat them. Although Conrad personally disavowed any kinship with the thematic intentions of Dostoyevsky, Hewitt finds striking resemblances between them, especially when they deal with conceptualized evil. For Hewitt "Fidelity" in Conrad means fidelity to a concept of infidelity or hollowness. Kurtz's creed, "Exterminate all the brutes," would be an example of fidelity gone wrong or maimed by hollowness.

Albert Guerard probably does the best job on the difficulties of interpreting the main thrust of Conrad's meaning. After analyzing his personal novels and his letters, his prefaces and his autobiographies, Guerard concludes that there are a number of inner conflicts which must be considered in order to fully appreciate Conrad's universe of fidelity:

a) Conrad felt bound to the authoritarianism of the mariner tradition and yet was motivated by his fierce individualism.

b) Conrad loved action but had a predilection for passive reverie.

c) Conrad was extremely conservative politically but sympathized greatly with the poor and disenfranchised.

d) Conrad believed ethical matters were simple but was extraordinarily sensitive to the complexity of moral problems.

e) Conrad shared the rationalist's distrust of the unconscious but he was possessed by a psychological drive that made him search deeply into the subconscious for motivation.

f) He distrusted idealism and revered it.

g) He feared the effects of faith-destroying intellect but he was gifted with a deeply ironic scepticism.

h) Finally, Conrad declared his fidelity and commitment to law as above the individual but he also believed that the betrayal of the individual was the most deeply felt of all crimes.

In short, Guerard outlines the conflicts between "this conscientious man and his wayward imagination." If viewed as a result of these inner contradictions, Conrad's novels seemed forged out of a driving need to establish some kind of aesthetic decorum which would resolve his inner drives. Yet, Conrad analyzed from a psychoneurotic point of view, as Guerard would have it, is Conrad stripped of his devastating ability to create a reality of the torment and perverted ecstasy prevalent in the divided heart.

IMAGES AND SYMBOLS: Before the revealing episodes in all of his stories, Conrad puts his characters through a shadow or fog: in *Heart of Darkness* there is the dense, white fog just below Kurtz's station; in *Lord Jim* there is that dense, white fog before Brown starts his fatal trip down the river in Patusan; in *The Secret Sharer* the ship drives through the shadow of Koh-ring before it turns out toward the sea. Conrad uses the shadow and the fog, according to many critics, as his symbol of the unconscious. In each of these highly personal stories, Conrad works on two levels: both telling the adventure story and conducting an equally adventuresome descent into the subconscious.

Another artist and thinker, Carl Jung, also explored the significance of the subconscious and its influence on our lives. Jung believed that it was necessary for every man to reach into his subconscious, to explore and understand it, and what is more, to gain control of the subconscious, before he could successfully lead his conscious life. Thus before the climax of each of his novels, Conrad presents a descent into the subconscious and a struggle with it. From this point of view, Leggatt in *The Secret Sharer* is the alter ego of the young Captain and Kurtz in *Heart of Darkness* is the alter ego representing the dark forces of Marlowe's own subconscious. On an imagistic level, the alter-image of the fog, shadow or mist is light. Light stands for the conscious perception of those forces that govern our lives. Darkness stands for the destructive, primitively harbored urges that dominate our personality. The interspersal of light with the dark is Conrad's way of stating that man needs above all self-knowledge and this knowledge is tenebrously compounded.

Frederick Karl plots Marlowe's trip into the Congo as a trip into a modern version of hell. He identifies fifty separate images which are all concerned one way or another with hellish things. Death and decay infest the story throughout, futility is incessantly underscored, and metallic and inflexible substances are strewn about. Kurtz is defined as a Dantesque sort of devil whose bald head itself becomes an allied symbol of the ivory he collects. Karl claims that the accumulation of images, although only tangentially related to the main plot line, relate to a more general experience beyond the boundaries of the story. Conrad's imagistic use of language expands our vision of Kurtz and his small jungle empire. We see in him the hollowness of western society and the degradation its materialism has caused. Furthermore, Karl contends that Conrad's characters are all impelled by some illusion of personal grandiosity; in other words, people in Conrad's stories are busy painting reality over to suit their own needs. These characters follow a dream as if it were a reality. Once you accept this assumption about them, it becomes rational to accept Conrad's use of symbols and images to construct a world around them. He is merely matching the form to the content, using metaphor to clarify a metaphorical existence. One of the effects of this intense impressionism of images is to suggest that illusions exist for every man and that no one "sees" truly and as Robert Penn Warren has pointed out, illusion is necessary, "is infinitely precious, is the work of . . . human achievement, and is, in the end, his only truth."

SOCIAL PSYCHOLOGICAL CRITICISM: It is interesting to measure the particular orientation of a critic against his resulting criticism. In *Joseph Conrad: A Study in Non-conformity,* Osborn Andreas would have us believe that Conrad's major creations deal with the problems of individuals adjusting to a mass society. The individual is perceived as struggling against group pressures to conform and Conrad himself is seen as trying to emancipate himself from the neurotic coils of guilt which had been winding around him ever since he left Poland. I said before that it might be interesting to gauge a critic through his orienting esthetic, however, in some critics, the orientation is so limited that it confines the artist and his work to a pigeon-hole. This compartmentalization so distorts the perception of the literary work that it is difficult to realize that one is talking about the same novel. In the case of Andreas, psychological jargon and the overuse of social psychology delimits Conrad's meanings and robs him of his rich philosophic potential. Conformity may be one of Conrad's ideas but it is not his central thesis.

HEART OF DARKNESS AND THE CRITICS

EARLY CRITICS: GARNETT AND MASEFIELD: In the years 1902 and 1903, which witnessed the publication of Conrad's *Heart of Darkness,* Conrad criticism was in its infancy. However, even at this early date there was a considerable divergence of opinion about the artistic values of *Heart of Darkness*. Edward Garnett, ever alert to genuine talent, saw in this story a psychological masterpiece. It caught the variety of shadings in the white man's difficult and weird relations with the exploited savages of Africa: "it implies the acutest analysis of the deterioration of the white man's *morale*, when he is let loose from European restraint. . . ." Conrad's presentation artistically arranges sensations and sequences of action in order to signify the essential meaning and/or meaninglessness of the white man in uncivilized Africa. Masefield, on the other hand, was one of the first to find fault with Conrad's rhetoric. Claiming that Conrad showed a tendency towards the "precious," he indicts him for polishing his prose to such a finish that he obscures the message. Also, he does not believe that Conrad's central character, Kurtz, is entirely believable; too much has been sketched in to make the reader believe or sympathize with his predicament. Despite these disclaimers Masefield does acknowledge that Conrad's was a poetic temperament and his artistic expression was "trembling with beauty."

HAROLD R. COLLINS: In an essay published in *The Western Humanities Review,* Collins demonstrates that Kurtz and the helmsman share in the moral isolation caused by detribalization, while the cannibals do not. Kurtz facing the jungle unprepared, professing to bring enlightenment to "darkest" Africa, is himself deprived of enlightenment because he has been cut loose from his tribal ways—he loses his European moral structure. The swaggering helmsman is an example of the effects of partial detribalization. He would like to behave like the white man and does indeed share a certain kinship with his white master, Marlowe. Nevertheless, at the crucial attack on the river-boat, he cannot discard his tribal heritage; he reverts to an old African war dance thus throwing his own life away and endangering the entire crew.

The cannibals are not yet defiled by contact with the white man. Collins feels that the cannibals may be morally indefensible— they eat people—but they are not "isolates." He quotes Diedrich Westermann's description of the social conditions of the un-civilized African in *The African Today and Tomorrow*: "The consciousness of being a well protected member of a group gives the individual a definite . . . dignity. . . . He knows no crawling humility, no slavish flattery, and he is not easily embarrassed. Within his own circle he is never in a position when he does not know how to behave or what to do." It is for these reasons that Marlowe remarks about their "dignified and profoundly pensive attitude." When Kurtz opens his mouth as if to swallow the entire universe, he demonstrates a cannibalism of quite a different order—a morally desperate voracity. While Kurtz and the helmsman are destroyed by the effects of detribalization, the cannibals traveling as they do with their society intact can survive.

MARLOWE'S FUNCTION: In an essay printed in *From Jane Austen to Joseph Conrad* W. Y. Tindall defends Conrad's use of Marlowe as aesthetically correct. F. R. Leavis found Conrad's story marred by Marlowe's excessive talking. When Marlowe is around, Leavis felt that Conrad had abdicated the "objective correlative" so necessary to support the narrative progress of events: Conrad becomes "intent on making a virtue out of not knowing what he means." Tindall claims that Marlowe has a double function—to serve the interests of realism as well as those of aesthetic distance. Marlowe functions as a Jamesian "central intelligence" through whom the reader gets an interpretation of what is transpiring in the story. Since Marlowe is both reporter and agent to the event, we receive a subjective truth entirely compatible with Conrad's belief that for the most part truth is inscrutable and illusion governs human affairs. In his very "long-windedness" Marlowe reveals the central realities of the story he has been said to mar. We as readers must make the distinction between Conrad, the reporter, and Marlowe, the interpreter. Once we have identified the several strains of character and attitude unique to Marlowe, we can share with him his discovery of self. Without Marlowe, Conrad might be guilty of a more heinous crime than verbosity, namely, the sin of didacticism which is fatal to the work of art. That is, without the sometimes illuminating and sometimes interfering refractions of Marlowe's thoughts, nothing would stand between us and "the message."

KURTZ IS HOLLOW AS PERSUASIVE FICTION: Echoing Masefield somewhat, Marvin Murdick in an essay published in *The Hudson Review,* "The Originality of Conrad," attacks the creation of Kurtz as a believable character. Murdick states that Conrad has not justified all the fuss he has made about Kurtz since when we do get to know him, he is revealed through pat, insubstantial irony. This is wholly insufficient documentation for the "universal genius" who has become cosmically degenerate.

The final scene between Marlowe and the Intended comes in for a great deal of adverse criticism from Murdick. He feels that it is composed of "cheap irony" and is full of "melodramatic tricks," especially when Marlowe describes emotional changes through sighs and heart palpitations. However, Murdick does recognize Conrad's great contribution as the writer who established that meaning in a work of fiction must be inherent in every recorded sensation: "After *Heart of Darkness,* the recorded moment—the word—was irrecoverably symbol."

MYTHIC AND EPIC PARALLELS: Marlowe's heroic search and the essentially tragic implication of his discovery have encouraged critics to assign literary parallels between *Heart of Darkness* and certain classical and archetypal journeys. Conrad's compulsive ambiguity and usage of symbolism have contributed to the wide divergence of the resulting parallels. Jerome Thale, for one, writing in *University of Toronto Quarterly,* July, 1955, likens

Marlowe to the knight in a medieval quest. He sees Marlowe's search for Kurtz as the knight's search for the holy grail and the illumination it can provide. Thale connects the grail motif with the profuse light-dark symbolism. Even though what Marlowe finds in the heart of darkness is even darker than present knowledge, he still achieves a form of illumination—self knowledge.

Recently, Lillian Feder, in an essay printed in *Nineteenth-Century Fiction, IX,* has pointed out a number of significant parallels with Virgil's descent in the sixth book of the *Aeneid.* Hades and the jungle are to Miss Feder legendary rather than actual underworlds and Marlowe's descent is termed an ideological rather than an actual immersion into hell.

Robert O. Evans disputes Feder's analogy with Virgil's source work. For him the important ideas in the *Heart of Darkness* find their true source in Dante's *Inferno.* Although he concedes that certain of Conrad's devices are shared by myths in general, he sees the underlying pattern of the story as a skeletonized version of the *Inferno.* He refers in particular to the concept of the Vestibule, the idea of the Limbo, the Nether Hell, the City of Dis and the Satanic inner circle. Evans uses the parallel with Dante to demonstrate that Conrad uses a variety of "epic" devices to insure that the reader achieves a certain kind of emotional freedom and is not retarded in his responses.

In "The Lotus Posture and 'The Heart of Darkness' " by William Stein, still another parallel is advanced—the similarity of Marlowe's discovery with the ideal of dispassionate Buddhahood. Regarding Marlowe's adventure as essentially a spiritual discipline, Stein sees Marlowe's journey as breaking free from the limits his own flesh imposes. What Marlowe discovers in the heart of darkness is the "way of the Bodhisattva." He discovers the suffering he has endured while being attached to external matter and he emerges from his own hell into the ascetic ideal, purified and cleansed of all earthly materialistic attachments. Although the evidence for this spiritual consecration is meagre, Stein finds the frame of the story not dependent on any "epic" technique. Indeed, to read this story as a development in Christian ego-strength would be to distort the mockery of the Christian underworlds displayed by Marlowe's ironic attitude.

THE SECRET SHARER AND THE CRITICS

CURLEY'S VIEW: Daniel Curley, in an essay published in *Conrad's Secret Sharer and the Critics,* defines this story as belonging to a type called "initiation-ritual." He sees Leggatt as an ideal personality who has not been homicidally impelled. Rather, the reverse is true; Leggatt has demonstrated superb self-understanding and typifies the kind of moral strength that the Captain aspires to achieve. By replicating Leggatt's initiation into self-confident manhood, the Captain actively manifests his mastery of the test of initiation.

CARL BENSON: Benson finds difficulty with accepting the version of *The Secret Sharer* as a complete initiation. In his article, "Conrad's Two Stories of Initiation," Benson compares this story unfavorably with another Conrad short story, *The Shadow Line.* Benson thinks that at the end of *The Secret Sharer* the Captain does not really understand the full nature of his communal duties. True, he has mastered himself in a limited egocentric way but he has not shown that he has achieved more than a perfunctory establishment of his authority as ship's captain. In *The Shadow Line,* Benson finds that Conrad has prolonged and intensified the nature of the initiation test. Perhaps the most important factor in complicating the process of testing is the insertion of an opportunity to feel remorse for the crew. By linking the Captain with the crew, Conrad has linked him with a wider human solidarity. What really happens in *The Secret Sharer,* and Benson makes sure the reader recognizes he is not trying to minimize its artistic power—is that the Captain has become aware of his own self—a necessary stage *before* he can become aware of how much that self is limited and developed by the community.

WALTER F. WRIGHT: In a section from his book, *Romance and Tragedy in Joseph Conrad,* Walter Wright identifies a Christian motif as the source of the thematic meaning of *The Secret Sharer.* Specifically, he calls attention to the motif of the kind act saving the doer. You will recall that in a burst of tenderness the Captain has given Leggatt his hat to protect him from the sun. This impulsive donation in turn works to prevent the Captain's ship from being destroyed. Wright finds that although Conrad disliked Tolstoy's belief in Christianity as a base for his art, he himself, as demonstrated by the gift in this story, used Christian ethics to climax *The Secret Sharer.* In Christian tragedy the hero achieves a form of expiation of his guiltiness when his own sin makes him pity others. As a result of his feeling of kinship and pity for Leggatt, the Captain compassionately offers the hat, thereby furnishing grounds for his communion with the crew—in other words, communion with life at large.

ESSAY QUESTIONS AND ANSWERS

1. Discuss religious allusions in Conrad's stories.

ANSWER: Conrad chooses images from Christian, classical, and Eastern religions. These images, in turn, fall into three classifications, regardless of their original source. First, and foremost, Conrad uses the classical device of a descent into Hell. Second, he follows the traditional Christian pattern of the quest. Finally, he uses the figure of the god made into man, the avatar, which occurs in all religions.

The pattern of a descent into Hell is most clearly seen in *Heart of Darkness*. The pattern is used in Homer's *Odyssey* and in Virgil's *Aeneid*. The hero of the tale must descend into Hell to discover some piece of information that is extremely important to him. The only person who can provide this information is the "shade" of a former friend or relative. The journey into Hell is dangerous and filled with perils on all sides. Once in Hell, the hero finds a misty, clouded scene. If he meets people, they usually appear vague and indistinct to him. The parallel with the *Heart of Darkness* is fairly clear—Marlowe thinks of Kurtz as a *voice*. When he finally does reach Kurtz, Marlowe talks to him for several days, until Kurtz dies. Kurtz's final message to Marlowe is relayed like the messages in classical myth—it is horrific and ambiguous. Finally, the scene in the interior jungle is sufficiently "Hellish" to satisfy us: the shrunken heads mounted on posts before Kurtz's house, the strange "ceremonies" in which Kurtz and the natives indulge, the witch doctors standing on the shore-line as Kurtz leaves, and most of all, the dense, white fog that envelops the river-boat just before it reaches Kurtz's station.

The pattern, then, is complete: the dangerous voyage within, the mists and fogs of Hell, the asking for information, and the final message itself.

"Quest" is a literary term for search, with some special implications. Perhaps the most famous of all quest stories is the search for the Holy Grail. In the Middle Ages, knights believed that the chalice from which Christ drank still existed. Many knights went off in search of the chalice or grail. Thus a quest is a searching after something of considerable importance; and successfully finding the object would bring special powers and grace to the hero. A typical theme in modern literature is a quest for a father, a theme used by James Joyce in his great novel *Ulysses*. The necessary elements of the quest include an object to be discovered, the trip of discovery itself, and the enlightenment at the end. *The Secret Sharer* offers us a good example of such a pattern. At the beginning of the story, the young Captain confesses that he is a stranger to his ship and to himself. His voyage, then, will be to discover both himself and the world around him. His voyage is filled with danger, the danger of discovery of his second self, Leggatt, by the crew of the ship. In the second part of the story, the release of Leggatt and the course of the ship through the shadow of Koh-ring is dangerous too. The young Captain succeeds in meeting this test of his self-command, and of his seamanship, with the help of his hat, the Jungian symbol for the integrity of the personality. Of course, the hat can also be the Christian symbol of the act of kindness which works to redeem the giver.

The avatar occurs primarily in the figure of Kurtz. In the *Heart of Darkness* he is presented as a universal genius appearing to the native as a God/man. His supernatural attributes are repeated over and over again; he is both too good and too bad for living in this world. He may be looked upon as the compendium of the Old Testament and the New Testament Gods. Wise and Satanic by turns, he offers Marlowe an insight into the divided nature of man and perhaps of man's supernal image —God.

Conrad uses the religious allusions to give structure and order to his tales, and to extend their rich significance These tales must not be read as pure religious allegories. They form along with the psychological probing and narrative action an organic testament about the moral structure of the universe.

2. Why does Marlowe lie to Kurtz's Intended?

ANSWER: Critics have offered many interpretations of Marlowe's lie. K. A. Bruffee considers the lie an example of Marlowe's newly won moral restraint. Inasmuch as the truth can conceivably destroy the Intended's illusion of Kurtz along with the Intended herself, Marlowe decides that his lie is situationally ethical and preferred to a truth which might be destructive.

However this view does not consider Conrad's attitude toward women and the dark information he has received from Kurtz. As a result of his quest Marlowe has discovered that the complete truth is black indeed. In his identification with Kurtz, Marlowe perceived that the soul of man has infinite capability for Satanic excesses. In our subliminal nature, if we can ever get in touch with it, lies a primitive savagery that is sinister and horrific. Upon contact with this debasing illumination, Marlowe falls deathly ill; he is spiritually paralyzed. When he returns to Brussels, he regards the populace with a cosmic contempt: "They were intruders whose knowledge of life was to me an irritating presence, because I felt so sure they could not possibly know the things I knew."

Furthermore, Marlowe's lie to the Intended is really the last of three lies he tells. The first occurs when he refuses to disabuse Kurtz's cousin of the notion that Kurtz was a "universal genius." The second occurs when Marlowe gives the journalist the report, "Suppression of Savage Customs," with the postscript ripped off. These might be termed lies of omission where Marlowe has

amended the truth rather than embroidered or deliberately mis-
represented it. In order to preserve the inferior community from
the searing truth of Kurtz, he has left them in ignorance. As
Marlowe tells his third lie perhaps we might say that unlike the
first two he is not interested in protecting society from the truth,
but rather he is trying to protect his own conception of truth.
He has admitted to a romantic notion about women. In discussing his aunt, Marlowe says, "They live in a world of their own,"
and "It's queer how out of touch with truth women are."
Nevertheless, they have a capacity for survival that males lack,
and, furthermore, they can suffer and still maintain their fidelity
and belief systems. The Intended is described by Marlowe as
having a "mature capacity for fidelity, for belief, for suffering."
Marlowe lies to her differently from the others. He intentionally
misrepresents Kurtz's last words. He explains that telling her
the truth "would have been too dark—too dark altogether." Since
Marlowe is so spiritually deflated by his contact with Kurtz,
isn't he lying to preserve his belief in the one human fact that
preserves us all—the invincible spirit of woman? Conrad seems
to be saying that if the truth vanquishes the female principle,
then we are all destroyed. Rather than cut himself off from all
illusion, Marlowe lies and remains, as the last words of the story
indicate, in "the heart of an immense darkness."

3. Describe the use of imagery in *The Secret Sharer*.

ANSWER: There is no universal agreement as to the meaning
of the word "imagery"; it is best to describe the different meanings that may be applied to the term, and then to show how
these various kinds of imagery operate in *The Secret Sharer*.
The most widely accepted meaning of the word "imagery" is
figurative or metaphoric language, especially ornamental language. Implied in this version of figurativeness would be the
analysis of diction, i.e., word choice, as well as sensual "pictures"
delivered through the word choice. Louis Leiter has done the
best job of analyzing the "image cluster" in this story. Textual
analysis of the first-section reveals images which suggest "in-
sanity," "mystery," and "moral obtuseness," and Leiter suggests
that we must correlate the clusters with the development of the

theme of self-knowledge. The setting at first is represented as mysterious and unknown ("half-submerged," "incomprehensible," "crazy of aspect"). As the narrator gets to know himself and what Leggatt has come to reveal to him, the images change to words of illumination ("silvery," "phosphorescence," "light," "astonished").

Another interpretation of the meaning of the word "imagery" is an enlarged one; it includes the symbolic meanings latent in the perceived picture. For instance, the pagoda and the tug which appear at the beginning of the story can be seen as foreshadowing symbols of the mountain of Koh-ring and the taking of the ship into land. The land which the tug heads for is described as "impassive," and the tug gets lost behind the hill of the great pagoda. That is, until we become involved in the search for self-hood, we cannot see the solid earth of our personalities. Leggatt sees himself as a Cain, a kind of a scapegoat thrown out of society. The Captain sees Leggatt as a double image of himself, the secret sharer of his unconscious life. When we begin to examine the word clusters and the symbolic clusters cooperatively, we can apprehend Conrad's descriptive technique—in which the word itself became "irrecoverably symbol." Images, what we see, and meaning, what we understand, are organized in such a way as to implement both the factual reality of the story and its thematic extension. There is a continuous working backward and forward between the concrete and the theoretical, between the real and the abstract: the proud swimmer, metaphorically and literally, strikes out for a new destiny.

4. Discuss Joseph Conrad's use of specific detail.

ANSWER: One of Joseph Conrad's greatest talents was his use of the minute, specific detail in order to suggest a general truth. This technique can be seen in his description of the Harlequin in *Heart of Darkness*. When Marlowe first encounters him all he sees are a bundle of sense impressions: his clothes are made of "brown holland," his suit is covered with patches, "bright patches, blue, red, and yellow—patches on the back, patches on elbows, on knees; colored binding round his jacket. . . ." The description of the details of the Harlequin's clothing leads to a minute description of his face and finally to some kind of evaluation of his personality. Conrad used this kind of descriptive technique to ensnare the reader's belief and persuade him to inner judgments about the character and/or event. According to Conrad himself, his overriding purpose as an author was to make his audience "see." He meant this vision to be on as many levels as possible. He used the means of vivid, specific sensory detail for the purpose of seducing the reader into perceiving an inner vision.

5. What was Conrad's attitude toward women?

ANSWER: Women are conspicuously absent from *The Secret Sharer*. They do not play a part in the narrative action nor are they referred to in passing. In the *Heart of Darkness* they do appear but somehow they are not very clearly drawn. First there is Marlowe's aunt who helps him to get his job. There are two women sitting in the "sepulchral city" knitting black wool when Marlowe appears for his interview. There is the magnificent native woman who loves Kurtz, and there is Kurtz's "Intended," whom both we and Marlowe meet at the end of the tale. At the beginning of the story Marlowe, speaking of his aunt, has remarked, "It's queer how out of touch with truth women are." When we consider another of Marlowe's statements, that there is nothing that he hates so much as a lie, and when we consider his final lie to Kurtz's "Intended," we begin to get an interesting picture of Marlowe's attitude toward women. They are at once to be protected from the truth and to be denied it. Perhaps Conrad wants to preserve their stainless illusion so that they can minister to men who have had their illusions and idealism shattered by reality.

BIBLIOGRAPHY AND GUIDE TO
FURTHER RESEARCH

I. CONRAD'S MAJOR WORKS: (with original date of publication in book form)

Almayer's Folly (1895)

An Outcast in the Islands (1896)

The Nigger of the "Narcissus" (1897)

Tales of Unrest (1898)

Lord Jim (1900)

Youth (1902) (This volume contained *Heart of Darkness*.)

Typhoon (1903)

Nostromo (1904)

The Mirror of the Sea (1906)

The Secret Agent (1907)

Under Western Eyes (1911)

A Personal Record (1912)

'Twixt Land and Sea (1912) (This volume contained *The Secret Sharer.*)

Chance (1913)

Victory (1915)

The Shadow Line (1917)

The Arrow of Gold (1919)

The Rescue (1920)

Notes on Life and Letters (1921)

The Rover (1923)

Tales of Hearsay (1925)

Last Essays (1926)

II. BIBLIOGRAPHY:

Beebe, Maurice. "Criticism of Joseph Conrad: a Selected Checklist," *Modern Fiction Studies,* I, February, 1955; 30-45.

Keating, George T. *A Conrad Memorial Library*. New York, 1929.

Lohf, Kenneth A., and Sheehy, Eugene P. *Joseph Conrad at Mid-Century; Editions and Studies*. 1895-1955. Minneapolis, 1957.

III. BIOGRAPHY:

Baines, Jocelyn. *Joseph Conrad*. New York, 1960.

Jean-Aubry, Gerard. *Joseph Conrad, Life and Letters*. London, 1927.

Gordon, John D. *Joseph Conrad: The Making of a Novelist*.

IV. CRITICISM—BOOKS:

Guerard, Albert, Jr. *Conrad the Novelist*. Cambridge, Mass., 1958.

Harkness, Bruce. *Conrad's Heart of Darkness and the Critics*. California, 1960.

———— *Conrad's Secret Sharer and the Critics*. California, 1962.

Karl, Frederick R. *A Reader's Guide to Joseph Conrad*. New York, 1960.

Leavis, F. R. *The Great Tradition*. London, 1948.

Stallman, R. W., ed. *The Art of Joseph Conrad, A Critical Symposium*. Michigan, 1960.

Van Ghent, Dorothy. *The English Novel: Form and Function*. New York, 1953.

V. CRITICISM—ARTICLES:

Collins, Harold P., "Kurtz, the Cannibals, and the Second-Rate Helmsman," *Western Humanities Review* VIII, Autumn, 1954; 299-310.

Evans, Robert O., "Further Comment on 'The Heart of Darkness,' " *Modern Fiction Studies, III,* Winter, 1957-58; 358-360.

Feder, Lillian. "Marlowe's Descent into Hell," *Nineteenth-Century Fiction,* IX, March, 1955, 280-292.

Gross, Seymour. "A Further Note on the Function of the Frame in 'Heart of Darkness'," *Modern Fiction Studies,* III, Summer, 1957.

Leiter, Louis. "Echo Structures: Conrad's 'The Secret Sharer'," *Twentieth Century Literature,* V, January, 1960; 159-175.

Murdick, Marvin. "Conrad and the Terms of Modern Criticism," *The Hudson Review,* Autumn, 1954; 419-426.

Stein, William Bysshe. "The Lotus Posture and 'The Heart of Darkness'," *Modern Fiction Studies,* II, Winter, 1956-57.

Zabel, M. D. "Introduction to *The Portable Conrad.*" New York, 1947.

SUGGESTIONS FOR RESEARCH PAPER TOPICS

1. Trace Conrad's influence on modern writers.

2. A study of the pattern of descent and emergence in *The Secret Sharer.*

3. The use of multiple narrators in *Heart of Darkness.*

4. The use of dialogue in *Heart of Darkness.*

5. Comparison of Kurtz with Albert Schweitzer.

6. Transitions between outer and inner reality.

7. Color as symbol.

8. The function of ambiguity.

9. The concept of fidelity.

10. Truth means alienation.

11. Truth means communion.

12. Illusion is the dominant reality.

13. Sensual experience as the prime agent of truth.

14. The ship: a microcosm of society.

15. The *Cutty Sark* incident: Biographical source for *The Secret Sharer*.

16. Religious sources for *Heart of Darkness*.

17. An analysis of metaphors relating to light and dark in *Heart of Darkness*.

18. Conrad's use of minor characters for thematic illumination.

19. Conrad: a Victorian in disguise.

20. Individualism versus social commitment in *The Secret Sharer*.